SOMETHING NEW IN MODEL BOAT BUILDING

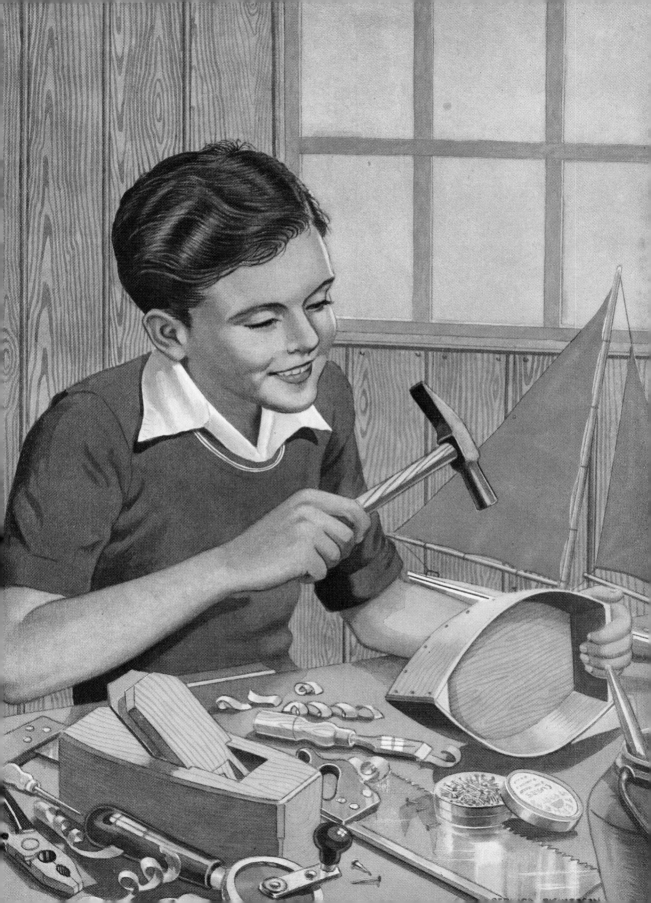

Something New in
MODEL BOAT BUILDING

*How to make Out-of-the Ordinary Model Boats
with Simple Tools and Materials*

by
DONALD H. MATHESON

Illustrated by
BERNARD RICHARDSON

HUTCHINSON'S
BOOKS FOR YOUNG PEOPLE
HUTCHINSON HOUSE
LONDON, W.1

Printed in Great Britain
by The Anchor Press, Ltd.,
Tiptree, Essex

CONTENTS

		Page
Chapter I	Tools and Materials	7
II	Hulls	9
III	A Catboat	14
IV	A Thermostatic Boat	18
V	A Model Power Submarine which dives and comes up again	22
VI	A South Sea Island Outrigger Canoe	25
VII	A Tension Motor Speedboat	29
VIII	A Lee-Board Sailing Boat	33
IX	A Simple Ferryboat	35
X	A Simple Jet-propelled Boat	38
XI	A Plank-section Sailing-Ship	41
XII	A Hydro Glider	44
XII	An Outboard Motor-Boat	47
XIV	A Simple Power Paddle-Boat	50
XV	A Yankee Clipper	53
XVI	A Model Power Warship	57
XVII	A Model Old-time Galleon	60
XVIII	A Rotor Ship	65
XIX	A Steam Turbine Boat	70
XX	An Electric Launch	73

LIST OF COLOURED ILLUSTRATIONS

Frontispiece

Submarine *facing page* 22

Plank-Section Sailing Ship 34

Galleon 60

Electric Launch 70

CHAPTER I

TOOLS AND MATERIALS

MAKING and sailing boats of all kinds is ever a favourite hobby with both young and old, for with the sea all around us, we are naturally interested in everything to do with water craft.

All the models given in this book may be made with ordinary tools and materials. These tools include hammer, pliers, screwdriver, knife, handsaw, scissors, padsaw, fretsaw, a couple of files (medium and rough), tin shears (or an old pair of scissors will answer quite well), gimlet, small plane and a spokeshave. Also a vice is very useful, and a fine-toothed hacksaw is certainly a welcome addition. Some sandpaper—grades 0, $1\frac{1}{2}$ and 2. Some of the models call for a small hand-drill, but even an Archimedean drill with bits will serve the purpose. However, a small soldering set is necessary if the construction of the electric, thermostatic and steam turbine models in particular are to be undertaken.

All the above may be purchased at modest cost from second-hand stores dealing in tools. Ex-Government disposal stores are the better places to try.

A variety of wire nails will be required (1 in. long, both oval and round); tacks, both gimp and tin-tacks; pin-nails, or "panel-pins" as they are usually termed; and $\frac{1}{2}$-in. small oval and round nails. A variety of small screws, both brass and iron, are useful, being about $\frac{1}{2}$ in. to 1 in. long.

It is a good plan to keep different nails, tacks and screws in empty glass jars or pots, such as fish-paste pots, jam-jars and the like. The contents can then be seen at a glance.

Some muslin, light calico or similar cloth for sails, and twine, or Strutt's Macrame, will be required. Also a compass, foot-rule and pencil, some elastic or rubber strands, cardboard, plywood, pieces of $\frac{1}{2}$ in. thick deal or similar wood, and some lengths of dowels, $\frac{1}{4}$ and $\frac{1}{2}$ in. diameter, a gluepot, and brushes, as well as varnish, including copal varnish; some stout wire and a lump of putty.

Plywood, dowels for masts, and in

7

fact all the wood necessary, may be obtained at woodworkers' stores, and also may be seen advertised for sale in "trade" papers.

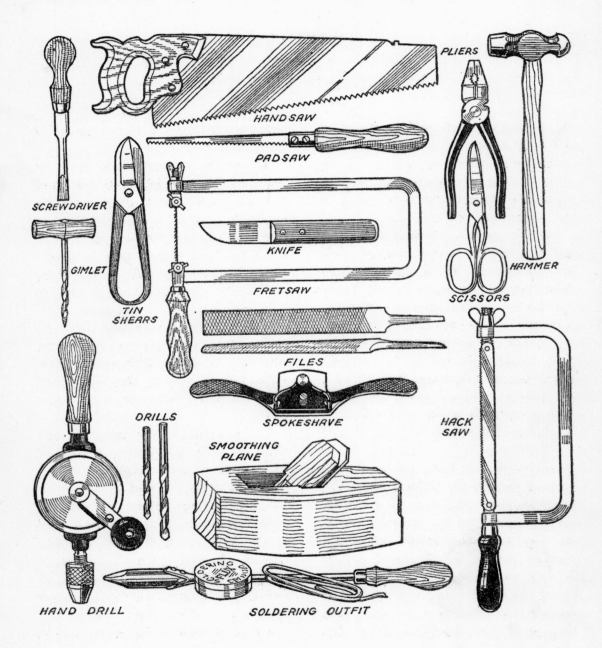

SCREWDRIVER

GIMLET

HAND SAW

PADSAW

TIN SHEARS

KNIFE

FRETSAW

FILES

DRILLS

SPOKESHAVE

SMOOTHING PLANE

HAND DRILL

SOLDERING OUTFIT

PLIERS

HAMMER

SCISSORS

HACK SAW

CHAPTER II

HULLS

USUALLY the hull of any boat is that part which requires first attention. There are several forms of construction suitable for the various craft described in this book, but most of the hulls are of the "flattie" type.

One method employs stout cardboard for the sides with wood bottom, the cardboard being treated, as will be shown, to make it durable and waterproof.

Commence by obtaining a sheet of cardboard of the brown "flexible" kind, as it is pliable and bends easily without cracking. It should be fairly stout, although the exact thickness is immaterial. If you can obtain some Essex Board, this will answer even better, being very stout cardboard.

Cut out two pieces to correspond with the length your boat is to be, and with the height in proportion, and tack to one end of these an angular bow-piece sawn from a piece of wood, as shown in the diagram. The other end of each of these sidepieces is tacked to the transom or sternpiece. You now have the sides of your hull shaped and secured. All that is needed is to place it on a piece of $\frac{1}{2}$-inch deal or suitable wood and

mark round inside with a pencil. Cut this out, place the sides over it, and tack around the bottom.

Now comes the process of making the cardboard impervious to water, and there are several ways of accomplishing this.

One method is to give it a good coat of glue on both sides of the cardboard and, when dry and hard, paint the hull both inside and outside. After the paint is dry, test how it floats. Any leakages at the joins should be stopped with putty. Now, having got your hull ready, you can carry on with making up the rest of the boat.

Another method of treating the cardboard to make it waterproof is with sealing-wax, of whatever colour you fancy. Break it by tapping with a hammer and place it in a bottle that has a neck large enough to permit the access of a paintbrush. Then cover the sealing-wax with methylated spirit, in which it will soon dissolve. Use this to "paint" the cardboard, and it will not only make it hard and impervious to water, but will dry hard and glossy, providing a very satisfactory finish.

You may, too, if you wish, use

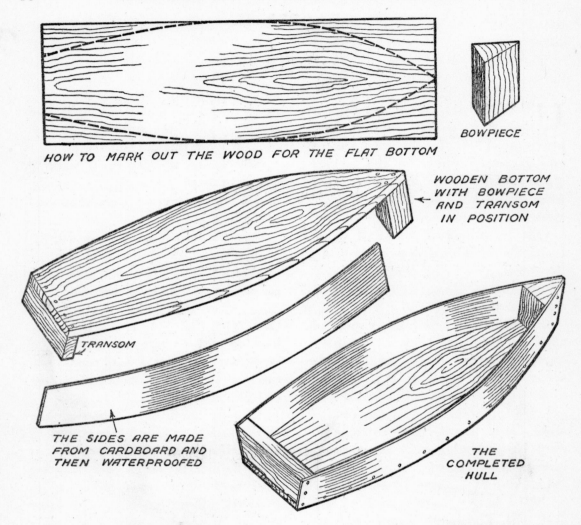

HOW TO MARK OUT THE WOOD FOR THE FLAT BOTTOM

BOWPIECE

WOODEN BOTTOM WITH BOWPIECE AND TRANSOM IN POSITION

TRANSOM

THE SIDES ARE MADE FROM CARDBOARD AND THEN WATERPROOFED

THE COMPLETED HULL

more than one colour, using a separate bottle for each colour, with, say, red sealing-wax dissolved in one bottle and green in another. The bottle containing the dissolved wax should be shaken until all is dissolved. If the resulting "paint" is too thick, add more methylated spirit. If too thin, add more wax. Of course,

if the sides are made from plywood, there is no need to treat for waterproofing.

Another good way to make a hull is to take a block of wood that is already shaped like a hull, or you may possess a purchased hull of a toy boat, probably one you have had a long time. Turn this over, laying it flat on your work-bench or table, and cover with calico, after first giving it a good rub over with cobbler's beeswax to prevent the calico adhering to the hull. Cut the cloth to coverings each glued over the other. When quite hard and dry, gently lift off the wooden hull, and you have a replica of that hull in calico, being stiff, durable and strong. All one has

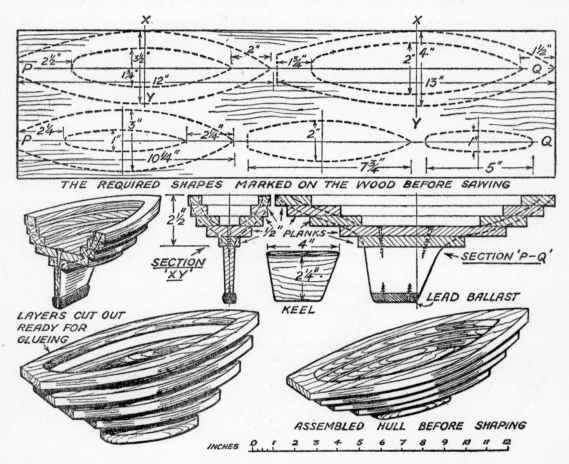

THE REQUIRED SHAPES MARKED ON THE WOOD BEFORE SAWING

SECTION 'XY'

½" PLANKS

KEEL

LEAD BALLAST

SECTION 'P-Q'

LAYERS CUT OUT READY FOR GLUEING

ASSEMBLED HULL BEFORE SHAPING

INCHES 0 1 2 3 4 5 6 7 8 9 10 11 12

fit over the hull all round. Thus you have your wooden hull neatly covered with calico. Give this a coat of glue and cover with another piece of calico, fitting over the whole. Allow to dry and then repeat the process until you have, say, six or more to do after trimming around the edges is to add finishing touches by means of paint and varnish. In fact, the better plan is to give the hull a coat of whatever colour paint you prefer and when dry add a finishing coat of copal varnish.

It is even possible to make quite a stout serviceable hull by using brown paper instead of calico, employing the same method.

One other way to make a hull, especially for sailing-craft, is by building it in "sections", the idea being to cut out a series of flat pieces of wood, cut to shape in decreasing dimensions. These, when nailed together, form the hull contour automatically, not so shapely or so smooth as a carved hull, perhaps, but this may be improved by means of knife, plane, spokeshave and sandpaper. Use as and where needed to improve the lines of the hull and smooth over all joins or edges of the wood sections after all are nailed together, using grade 2 sandpaper, followed finally by $1\frac{1}{2}$ and 0.

Quite an attractive model sailing-ship may be built in this way and the method is well worth trying—an excellent occupation for a wet afternoon. Dimensions are given on the diagrams, but you may make them proportionally larger or smaller, as required. Ordinary planking like deal, pine, elm, or even packing-case wood, may be used. If you also cut out the *inside* of each you'll then have a hollow hull, which is all to the good for a sailing-ship, as a hollow hull sails much keener than a block hull.

Yet another method is to hammer tin of suitable dimensions over a block of wood and to solder the

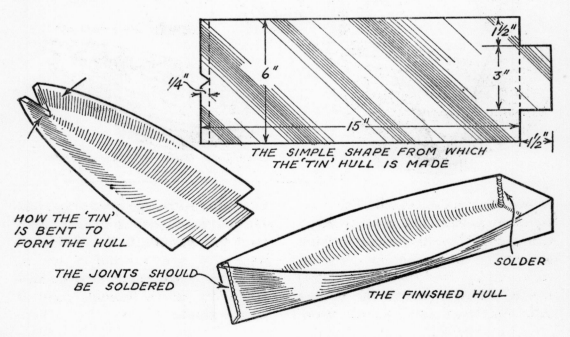

THE SIMPLE SHAPE FROM WHICH THE 'TIN' HULL IS MADE

HOW THE 'TIN' IS BENT TO FORM THE HULL

THE JOINTS SHOULD BE SOLDERED

SOLDER

THE FINISHED HULL

joints. This "tin" or metal hull answers excellently for hulls in which one uses a methylated spirit burner, as, of course, the metal is fireproof.

You may also cut out a shape in tin after the plan shown in the diagram and bend this into the form of a hull, soldering the joints as indicated in the illustration.

Unless otherwise stated, the construction of all the hulls described in the following pages conforms to one or other of the simple methods outlined in this chapter.

CHAPTER III

A CATBOAT

A CATBOAT has a wide beam in proportion to its length, is of shallow build with generous centre-board, and one big sail.

There are two ways in which the amateur may try his hand at making one of these jolly little craft. One is by having "planked" sides and the other is by modelling out of a block of suitable wood. The latter is, perhaps, the easier. But we will describe both ways and begin with the "planked-side" flattie type.

For this you will require a length of deal or elm planking 12 ins. long and 5 ins. wide and from about $\frac{1}{4}$ to $\frac{1}{2}$-in. thick. Shape into the form of a hull-bottom as shown in the diagram. The best method is to take a sheet of stout paper and cut with scissors to the same size—that is, 5 ins. wide and 12 ins. long, and double down the centre longways. Then draw half the outline in pencil. Cut out while keeping doubled over. On flattening out the paper again you have your 12 ins. by 5 ins. hull shaped similarly on either side, and have only to place this on the wood and mark round with a pencil and saw to shape. Use either a compass-saw, a pad-saw or a stout fretsaw.

Having shaped your hull and smoothed up the sawn edges, next obtain two lengths of thin plywood $1\frac{1}{2}$ ins. wide and somewhat longer than 12 ins., and tack with copper or galvanized tacks or small "pin-nails" to the edge of the flat wooden bottom, beginning with the bow and bending round towards the stern. Saw off that which projects beyond and then do the same to the other side. Next tack on your transom or stern-piece, using a piece of deal planking of the same kind and thickness as the bottom.

You now have your hull ready except for strengthening the bow. This is accomplished by tacking a piece of stout "wedge-shaped" wood inside the bow.

Next "deck-in" the top. Thin ply-wood is best for this and you will, of course, see just how to cut it to fit your hull. The diagrams show how it appears.

Before decking over the bow, however, tack a piece of wood cut from the $\frac{1}{2}$-in. planking of which the bottom is made across the hull from side to side $1\frac{1}{2}$ ins. from the bow. This is to take the mast, so it should be of strong material. A hole is made in the centre of this cross-piece to take the mast, and a "step" is made by boring a hole in a small block of wood

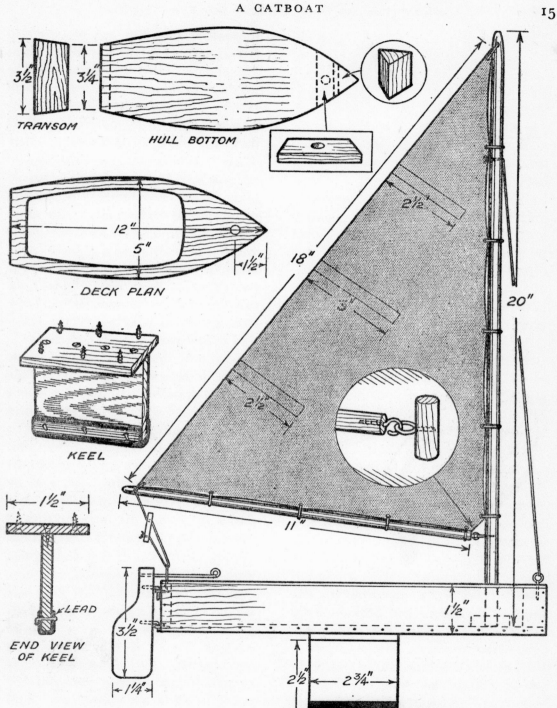

TRANSOM

$3\frac{1}{2}''$

$3\frac{1}{4}''$

HULL BOTTOM

DECK PLAN

12"

5"

$1\frac{1}{2}''$

KEEL

END VIEW
OF KEEL

$1\frac{1}{2}''$

LEAD

$3\frac{1}{2}''$

$1\frac{1}{4}''$

$2\frac{1}{2}''$

$2\frac{3}{4}''$

LEAD

$1\frac{1}{2}''$

$2\frac{1}{2}$

$18''$

$3''$

$2\frac{1}{2}$

$11''$

$20''$

LINES DRAWN TO
REPRESENT
DECK SEAMS

BENT
WIRE
'HORSE'

the sail is best cut out in paper to get a pattern first. The dimensions are given in the drawings. Care is needed in making a sail, but you will be able to make quite a good one out of some light, thin material such as muslin, calico, or any similar cloth. Three "sockets" or long thin pockets are made as shown, and these are to take three very light thin slips of wood. If you observe any of the man-carrying sailing-boats on river or sea, you'll notice that many have these artificial supports, as it were. If it were not for these slips of wood the sail would sag and not take full advantage of the wind.

The centreboard should next be made, and should be of thin wood $2\frac{3}{4}$ ins. long and $2\frac{1}{2}$ ins. deep. This is screwed or nailed with panel-pins to a piece of wood $2\frac{3}{4}$ ins. by $1\frac{1}{2}$ ins., which in turn is secured to the hull with tiny screws. The centreboard is weighted with lead as shown in the diagrams. This is to balance the boat, and the exact weight or amount of lead is best found by giving the boat a tryout. A piece of sheet lead about $\frac{1}{8}$ in. thick and bent to slip over the wood and secured with panel-pins is suitable.

A rudder is fitted to the stern and should be about $3\frac{1}{2}$ ins. long by $1\frac{1}{4}$ ins. wide and shaped as shown in the diagrams, with a tiller made from stout wire. The boat should be rigged, too, as shown, and you may paint it whatever colour you wish.

for the end of the mast to fit in. This step is tacked to the bottom of the boat directly below the cross-piece. (See diagrams.)

The mast should be about $\frac{3}{8}$ in. thick and 20 ins. long. A length of dowel will answer admirably, while

Before fitting the mast, rudder and centreboard, however, you should give the whole boat inside and out a good coat of paint, using, say, grey for the first coat, and, if any leaks occur, stopping them with putty, pressed on with a spatula or putty-knife, which will make all watertight. The second coat may be green or blue with a white or appropriate colour-line around the gunwale. A final coat or two of clear varnish should be given.

If you make your hull out of a suitable block of wood, see that you use light wood, preferably deal or pine, and made to the same dimensions—that is, 12 ins. long by 5 ins. wide and 1½ ins. thick, and cut and shape the same as the "planked-side" flattie. You will then have a solid hull instead of a hollow one. The mast, sail, boom, rudder and keel are all of the same dimensions. Try out first with mast and keel before fixing the sail and see how she takes the water. If she is leaning a trifle to one side, pare away some of the wood above the waterline at that side until the balance is even. Before removing any wood, however, you should decide from where you are going to take it, remembering that wood removed from above the waterline, or from the inside in the case of a hollow hull, will lighten the side of the craft from which the wood is taken. On the other hand, wood carved from the outside of the hull *below* the water-line will have the opposite effect, since the effective lift in water of the wood which has been removed will be absent.

If, on fitting the mast, you find the boat seems a bit top-heavy, shorten the mast a trifle by cutting a piece off the top. If necessary, a heavier piece of lead may be fitted to keep the boat steady. It is a good plan to make a temporary sail out of, say, stout paper and tie or fit to the mast with drawing-pins and so give the whole craft a good try-out. Then, by blowing vigorously at the sail, you can note whether the sail and mast are too much for the hull, and also whether the keel and ballast are sufficient. A solid hull needs a little more trying out than a hollow hull. The craft should rock from side to side up to about 45° when blown at, yet not capsize.

Mark a line about ¼ in. wide around the top of the hull with white paint, and use, say, jade green for the rest of the hull with red for keel, employing a white sail. An alternative colour scheme is shown on the cover of this book. Rig the boat in the same way as the hollow one, using either brown fishing-line or Strutt's Macrame.

These catboats are excellent sailers and very popular. They employ only the one sail, hence are sometimes referred to as mono-sailers or mono-type catboats. Either solid hull or hollow-type are easy to make by anyone handy with tools, while the cost is negligible.

B

CHAPTER IV

A THERMOSTATIC BOAT

A THERMOSTATIC boat employs a very old idea. The "power" or forward urge is acquired by means of water which is heated in a small boiler and automatically ejected through a pair of tubes leading from the boiler and out through the stern, thereby driving the little boat ahead with a "pop". Strange as it may appear, the same tubes also automatically suck back water again into the boiler, and thus the cycle of motions is repeated until the lamp is exhausted. The diagrams are simple and easy to follow and show just how to construct this type of craft.

The hull employed for this boat should be light in construction, about 9 to 12 ins. long with 3 to 4 ins. beam, but may be of more generous dimensions if desired. The flattie type of hull will do quite well and may be made by cutting out a flat piece of wood of about $\frac{1}{4}$ in. thick, in keeping with above dimensions, with a transom shaped as shown in the diagram.

The bottom of the boat should be covered with tin cut to shape and tacked down, thus making the bottom fireproof. The sides also should be made from thin tin. Empty tins may be utilized to obtain this material. You can, however, buy sheets of thin tinplate at an ironmonger's, and make

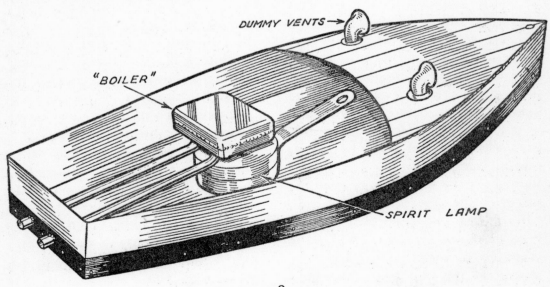

DUMMY VENTS →

"BOILER"

SPIRIT LAMP

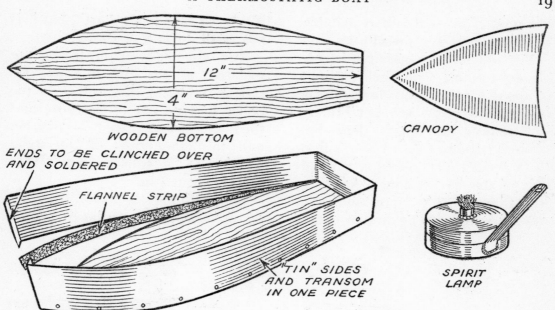

WOODEN BOTTOM

12"

4"

CANOPY

ENDS TO BE CLINCHED OVER
AND SOLDERED

FLANNEL STRIP

"TIN" SIDES
AND TRANSOM
IN ONE PIECE

SPIRIT
LAMP

the hull entirely of metal, soldering the joins. However, if you are going to use wood for the bottom, tin may then be used for the sides, and these should be tacked to the bottom with small tacks, using one to every half-inch. A strip of flannel should be run along the edge of the wood, with the tacks passing through tin and flannel. The flannel acts as water-tightener. The idea of using wood as a base to build your hull is to make it easier in fitting the tin sides. An all-metal hull would entail considerable soldering, whereas, with this method, no soldering is necessary, except at the bow and where the tubes are joined to the tin.

If you use sufficient length of tin, the same piece will reach all round the boat, being tacked to the bottom and clinched together at the bow, where the two ends meet. You may use thin wood for the sides if you wish, lining them with tin in the same manner as the bottom to make them fireproof. Also the transom may be made of wood covered with tin. The holes in the transom, through which the tubes project, should be at the bottom so that they are just submerged when the boat is afloat.

Having completed your hull, the next thing is to install the boiler. This may be made from an empty tin that has an airtight cover, or at any rate is so constructed that it can be made steamtight except for the two holes for the tubes. A flat type of tin is the more suitable, but practically any tin will do.

You will need to obtain two lengths of copper tubing, with a hole diameter of about $\frac{1}{8}$ in. It is not bound to be copper, however, as any metal tubing will suffice, the length depending upon the distance your boiler is from the transom. You may get a rough idea of this by bending a length of wire from boiler to stern, and upon straightening it out again thus obtain

if you are new to the "art", but it is not at all difficult or complicated.

The other ends of the tubing are soldered to the tin transom. Of course, soldering the tubes to the boiler is done out of the boat and then the boiler placed in position and the other ends of the tubes soldered to the transom, where they project about $\frac{1}{4}$ in.

A spirit-lamp is made from an empty ointment or similar tin with a

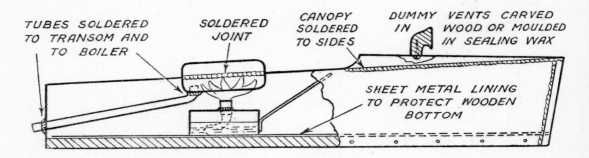

TUBES SOLDERED TO TRANSOM AND TO BOILER — SOLDERED JOINT — CANOPY SOLDERED TO SIDES — DUMMY VENTS CARVED IN WOOD OR MOULDED IN SEALING WAX — SHEET METAL LINING TO PROTECT WOODEN BOTTOM

your dimensions. These two lengths of tubing are fitted snugly into holes in the bottom of the boiler and about an inch apart. They have, of course, to be soldered. To accomplish this successfully, first clean the tin and tubing where the soldered joint is to be made and run or smear on a little soldering-flux (which may be purchased for a few pence), place some bits of solder on the joint and then, with a small-mouth blowpipe or soldering-iron, melt the solder until it runs around the joint. Soldering requires a little patience and practice

hole in the top. Into this is inserted and soldered a short length of copper tubing or piece of tin bent round into the form of a tube about $\frac{3}{8}$ in. diameter, and projecting about $\frac{1}{2}$ in. A length of tin about $\frac{1}{2}$ in. wide should be soldered at one side to serve as a handle for lifting in and out of the boat. Cotton wool saturated with methylated spirit is placed in the lamp with the cotton wool projecting about $\frac{1}{8}$ in. or so through the wick-channel.

A hood or canopy over the bow, made from tin and tacked to the woodwork of the sides if the sides are made from wood, or soldered if of metal, greatly adds to the appearance. The craft, too, may be painted whatever colour you choose.

This novel little boat affords a lot of fun and also serves a useful, instructive, scientific purpose.

To start the boat one has only to hold it stern upwards and pour some water into the tubes, thus supplying the boiler with water to start. Then, keeping your fingers over the outlets of the tubes, place the boat in the water. The tubes, being submerged, prevent the water running out again. Now place the lighted lamp under the boiler. The water, vapourizing into steam, which acquires pressure, drives the craft forward.

CHAPTER V

A MODEL POWER SUBMARINE WHICH DIVES AND COMES UP AGAIN

THIS model is very simple and easy to make. Commence by obtaining a length of round wood about 2 ins. in diameter. Any kind of wood will suit, provided it is not too heavy. Elm is too "solid", as, when wet, it increases in weight, which would hardly do for the purpose in view. Although a submarine is an underwater boat yet, if made of elm, it will have a tendency to remain awash all the time, especially after being fitted out. Deal is the more suitable, and if you are unable to procure a length of round wood of suitable dimensions, a piece sawn from some two-by-two deal will answer admirably. You may make the submarine any size, but 12 ins. long makes a very good model. Shape the wood into the contour of a cigar as shown in the diagram by the aid of plane, spokeshave and knife.

Smooth all over with sandpaper. Next cut the model in half lengthways, and shape out a groove on each half so that when placed together again a hole is formed about half an inch or so in diameter the entire length of the hull. Use a gouge, finishing with glass-

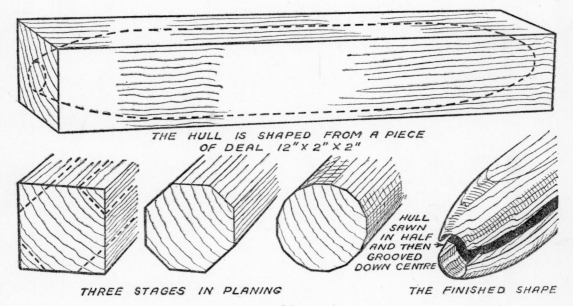

THE HULL IS SHAPED FROM A PIECE
OF DEAL 12" X 2" X 2"

HULL
SAWN
IN HALF
AND THEN
GROOVED
DOWN CENTRE

THREE STAGES IN PLANING

THE FINISHED SHAPE

BERNARD RICHARDSON

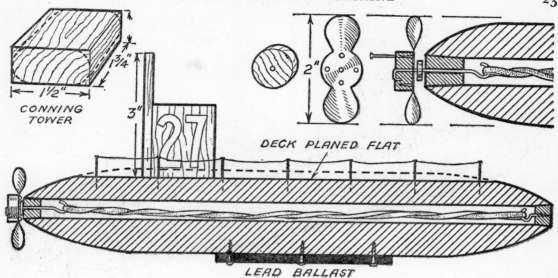

CONNING TOWER

3"

27

2"

DECK PLANED FLAT

LEAD BALLAST

paper, to make your groove, then fasten the two halves together again with brass screws. Next make the propeller, which should be 2 ins. in diameter, using a small piece of round wood for the hub, with the two-bladed propeller cut to shape from tin and tacked to it with small copper or galvanized tacks or small copper screws. A wood plug fits the propeller end of the hull and through this a hole is bored to form a "stern-tube" to take the shafting, the latter being a piece of stiff wire forced into a small hole in the propeller-hub and turned over into the wood again. The other end of the wire is bent into a loop to take the elastic power-strands. A 1-in. wire nail is partly tapped into the wooden hub near the edge, thus forming a handle for winding up the rubber motor, as shown in the

diagrams. A washer made from a small piece of lead makes an effective medium between propeller and "stern-tube". Two, four, or six strands of rubber or elastic are secured to the propeller shaft threaded through the length of the hull and fastened to the wire hook in the plug at the other end. It is easy to do this, as one may temporarily tie a piece of string to the rubber strands and thread through the hole in the hull, pulling the strands through after it, the ends of which are pulled out taut and dropped over the hook in the plug. This then fits back into the hull, being "snapped" in by the rubber tension. The elastic or rubber strands should be just taut when the propeller is stationary.

Lead ballast is screwed to the bottom of the hull, and should be of

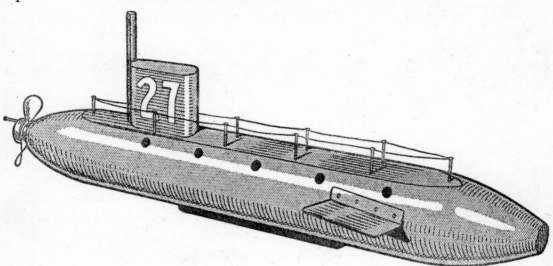

sufficient weight to half submerge the submarine when it is placed in the water. The conning tower is cut from an oblong block as shown in diagram, with a periscope made from a wooden skewer or similar piece of wood about 3 ins. long.

The diving apparatus which makes the submarine dive and come up again consists of two fins or vanes, one tacked or screwed at each side, and at a slight angle about 3 ins. from the bow and just below the waterline. They may be made of tin and about 3 ins. long and 1 in. wide.

The rubber motor is wound up by the key with the right hand, while the submarine is held in the left, and on being placed in the water the thrust of the propeller drives the submarine forward, while the angle of the fins causes the craft to take a down-ward slant. Upon the rubber motor running down, the submarine comes to the surface again, ready for another wind-up, with the journey repeated.

The craft should be painted grey, with black for the lead ballast, while the conning tower and periscope should also be grey, with black markings to represent portholes.

An added touch of realism may be given by making deck rails from pins and twine. The pins are pushed through the twine, which is forced up to the head of each pin before the pins are inserted in the hull. A spot of cellulose adhesive on each pinhead will keep the rails in position.

A name should be painted on the bow of the hull; or simply a number on the conning tower will do. All moving parts should be well vaselined. A study of the diagrams should make all clear.

CHAPTER VI

A SOUTH SEA ISLAND OUTRIGGER CANOE

THE South Seas are the home of the outrigger canoes, where the water is always warm, and the giant Pacific rollers come hurtling to shore with the speed of an express train, finally to expend their power in a lather of creamy foam on the sun-lit beaches.

To make a model after the style of one of these outriggers is quite easy for the amateur. The native South Sea outrigger is really a log of wood, dug out or hollowed out as much as possible; hence the word "dugout" is more often used relating to this type of craft, rather than canoe. But, of course, it is the "outrigger" that keeps the canoe from capsizing. This consists of a log of wood connected at a suitable distance from the canoe.

In making your model, commence with the hull or canoe part, and this may be made from a pine log 18 ins. long and about 2 ins. or less in diameter.

The hollowing-out takes time, but may be accomplished by the aid of a mallet and chisels, using a half-round gouge and square-tool. The log should be held steady while working on this, and so needs to be held in a vice, or even clamped to table or bench. Or, again, one may nail each end to a stout wooden bench or large piece of wood to hold it in position while hammering out the chips, the nails being left with their heads protruding so that they may be removed by the aid of pincers after completion of "digging out". This will not mar the "log", as each end should be sawn to a point, and the resulting holes left by the nails after withdrawing them can be filled in with putty.

All the parts to make this outrigger may be obtained from Nature. Saw off a "log" of the dimensions given for the canoe from a branch of a sycamore or fir tree, using smaller tree branches to supply the outrigger and its connecting arms. The masts, too, may be selected from thin sycamore branches, and the sail made from "matting"—like floor matting. If you can get a suitable piece of this cut from a mat that has been discarded it will do excellently. Or you may try your hand at weaving one, by intertwining bass or the flat straws used by gardeners. Or again, dried grass of the wide blade varieties that are to be found everywhere, may be utilized. Alternatively you may employ cloth. But if you do, use something coloured, like a discarded coloured handkerchief. This will

25

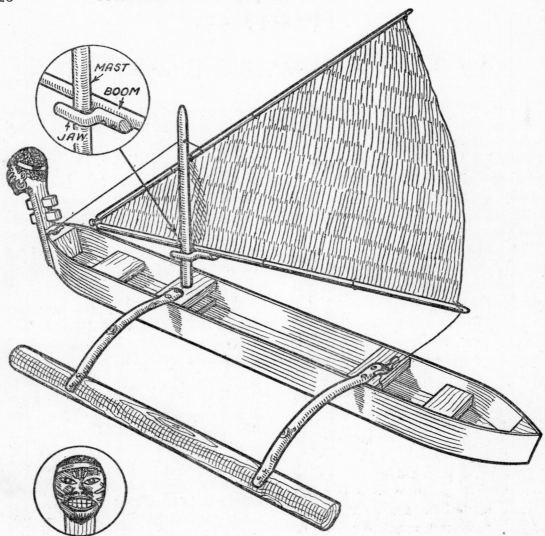

greatly add to the appearance and be more in keeping than a white sail, which is out of place on a South Sea Island outrigger canoe.

But perhaps you may wish to make up a hull and not have to dig it out. This may be accomplished by taking a piece of any light, ordinary wood, like deal or plywood, about $\frac{1}{4}$ in. thick, 18 ins. long and $1\frac{3}{4}$ ins. wide, and sawing both ends to a point, and tacking around the sides thin wood about $1\frac{1}{2}$ ins. wide. Veneer or thin plywood may be used for this. Or you may use stout cardboard, treating it as given in the chapter on hulls to make it impervious. A seat may be installed at each end.

The mast should be about $7\frac{1}{2}$ ins. long and about $\frac{1}{4}$ or $\frac{3}{8}$ in. thick. At the top a hole is drilled of sufficient size to permit thin twine or Strutt's Macrame twine to pass through it. This is for the halyard, which at one end is fastened to the yard to which the sail is tacked, the other end being wound round a cleat in the bow.

The sail is triangular in shape, being 10 ins. long at each side, while the two spars, yard and boom are 11 ins. long, or each about 1 in. longer than the sail. At one end of each spar is a small staple, or panel-pin, partly knocked in and bent half round to form a loop, and linked together by a small circle of wire to form a

hinge. The yard, on being hauled to the mast-peak by the halyard, then hangs or "sets" just right, with the boom in position. At one end of the boom is fastened a length of twine. This is called the "sheet", and wound round a cleat by the stern outrigger connecting-arm. A boom-stay is secured just where the boom rubs against the mast, half-circling the mast by means of a "jaw", made and shaped as shown in the diagrams. The mast passes through a hole in a thwart, in which it fits snugly, and down into a step-socket, this being a small block of wood secured to the bottom of the hull and with an $\frac{1}{2}$ in. hole, in which the mast fits.

Next, see to fitting the connecting-arms. These should be long enough to

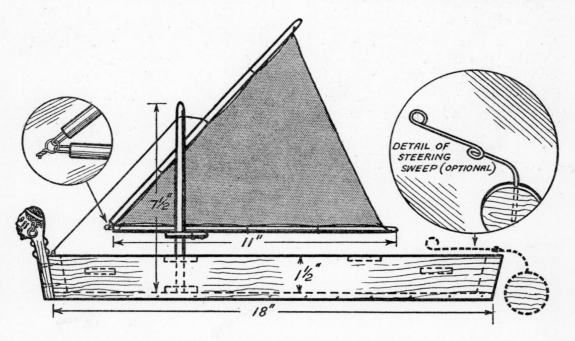

DETAIL OF STEERING SWEEP (OPTIONAL)

$7\frac{1}{2}$"

11"

$1\frac{1}{2}$"

18"

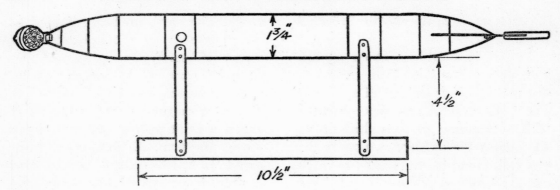

keep the outrigger about 4½ ins. distant from the canoe. These, too, are made from selected "branches" with the bark peeled off, and they should be slightly curved. You will want to ensure that the outrigger log balances the canoe, so it will be necessary, after tacking the connecting arms to the two thwarts in the canoe, to tie the connecting arms temporarily to the outrigger-log, which should be about 10½ ins. long and from ½ to 1 in. thick. The canoe should ride level with the log afloat and not lean over towards it, as it will if the outrigger is too heavy or too near the hull. When you have got all adjusted correctly, secure the cross-arms to the outrigger-log. The fore cross-arm has a length of twine connecting it to the bow.

Now give an artistic touch to your South Sea Island outrigger canoe by fitting a figurehead at the bow. This may be in the form of a grotesque human head fashioned in plastic wood, or in the form of a gargoyle or dragon. Alternatively it may be carved from a lump of plaster of Paris and afterwards varnished with shellac to make durable, then painted. Also on each side of the bow a fish, dolphin, or even a grotesque figure may be painted. This greatly adds to the artistic finish, and as regards colouring the canoe and outrigger, a dark stain looks well with a finishing coat of copal varnish. You may, however, use black on the canoe below the waterline and underside of bottom of canoe.

CHAPTER VII

A TENSION MOTOR SPEEDBOAT

A TENSION motor speedboat is another simple and easily made craft. The flattie type of hull is the more suitable and may be made with cardboard or Essex Board sides, treated to make waterproof, as described in the chapter on hulls or may be made of plywood or any thin wood.

Construct as in diagrams, commencing with the bottom, which may be made of thin wood or plywood,

24 ins. long and 7 ins. wide at its widest part. Tack on the sides with a stout sternpiece in deal, elm, or any suitable wood. A bow-strengthener is added as shown. A skeg block under the stern is secured with screws through the bottom of the boat, a hole having first been drilled through the block to take the stern-tube. This should be about 8 ins. long and may be of brass or any suit-

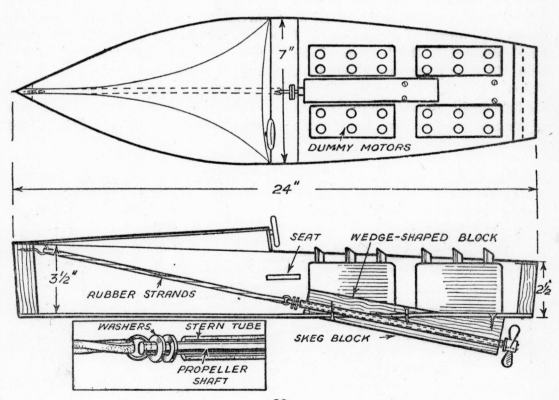

7"

DUMMY MOTORS

24"

3½"

SEAT   WEDGE-SHAPED BLOCK

RUBBER STRANDS

2½

WASHERS   STERN TUBE

SKEG BLOCK

PROPELLER SHAFT

able metal with a $\frac{3}{16}$ in. hole, through which the shafting is to pass. If you haven't a drill long enough to bore right through the skeg block, then you might try drilling first from one end and then from the opposite end. However, this calls for considerable skill to make the holes line up, and an alternative and equally effective arrangement consists of a bracket support for the rear end of the stern-tube. Details of a simple bracket made from a strip of sheet brass or tin are also shown in the illustrations.

You will need to make a hole in the bottom of the boat about 8 ins. from the stern for this tube to pass through, and it is then held securely in position by means of a small block of wood screwed to the bottom of the boat, the tube projecting about $\frac{1}{8}$ in. from the blocks at either end. Making the hole on an "incline" in the bottom of the boat requires care, but if made

too big the gap may be easily plugged around the tube-block with putty.

Through the stern-tube passes a propeller shaft 8 ins. long. The shaft may be any stout rod, such as brass, copper, or iron wire about $\frac{1}{8}$ in. diameter, and it should be an easy running fit, not a sloppy one, in the tube. It is worth while spending a little time in the selection of a suitable piece of tubing and shafting. One end of the shaft has the propeller soldered to it. And the propeller may be made, too, of any material, even cut from stout tin and afterwards painted with aluminium paint to prevent corrosion. It should be 2 ins. in diameter and have two blades. You may purchase a propeller about this size cast in brass all ready for soldering on to the shaft if you wish.

Having completed this, slip two washers over the shaft. These you may make yourself out of sheet lead

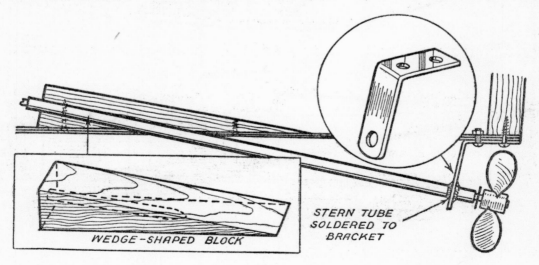

WEDGE-SHAPED BLOCK

STERN TUBE SOLDERED TO BRACKET

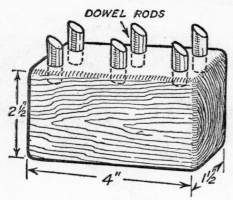

DOWEL RODS

$2\frac{1}{2}''$

$4''$ $1\frac{1}{2}''$

of the high-powered dummy motors. There are four of these, each representing 1,000 h.p., after the style of the pre-war international speedboat racers.

These motors are made from blocks of wood 4 ins. long, $1\frac{1}{2}$ ins. wide and $2\frac{1}{2}$ ins. high, and placed in position 1 in. from the sides of the hull and about 2 ins. away from the stern, with a space between of about 2 ins. Along the top of each are glued six $\frac{1}{2}$ in. long and $\frac{1}{4}$ in. diameter dowels or suitable round sticks such as wooden skewers, to represent the exhaust tubes, making twenty-four in all, as shown on the diagrams.

A narrow strip of tin about 1 in. wide and $3\frac{1}{4}$ ins. long is bent to cover the bow where the two sides meet, and secured with small panel-pins to the wooden bow-strengthener. This strengthens the bow-joint.

A short length of stiff, stout wire soldered to the middle of one of the

scrap, cutting small discs and making a hole in the middle to fit on the shaft. One of these washers is for the propeller end and the other for the front end. Here a hole is drilled through the shaft to take a small brass or iron wire ring. This ring can be made by bending a thin wire nail to the required shape. To the ring are attached the rubber tension strands. These may consist of 6 or 8 flat or round strips or strands of rubber, or elastic. The other end of these strands is attached to an eye-screw in the bow-block, as shown in the diagrams.

Next make the cover or hood, which should come down about half-way, or 12 ins. from the bow. This may be thin wood, tin, or even cardboard, with a crosspiece from side to side on which is fitted a dummy steering-wheel made from a round piece of wood, with a seat placed just behind it, while a stern crosspiece 1 in. wide is fitted as shown.

Next come the making and fitting

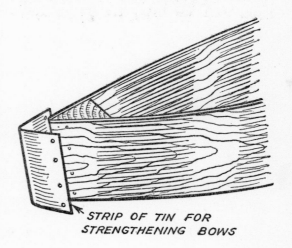

STRIP OF TIN FOR STRENGTHENING BOWS

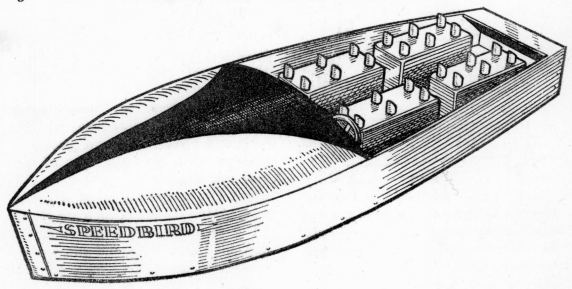

propeller-blades provides an effective "key" or handle for winding up the motor. Or one may easily wind up, using the forefinger of the right hand as a "key", while the boat is held in the left hand.

Regarding painting: green for the engine-blocks with aluminium exhaust-tubes, and red for the boat, looks well. Or black for the engine-blocks with aluminium exhaust-tubes and white for the boat is also attractive.

All moving parts should be well greased. It is also an advantage to lubricate the elastic or rubber strands with pure soft soap, or one of the preparations sold for this purpose. This prevents any likelihood of the strands adhering when under tension.

CHAPTER VIII

A LEE-BOARD SAILING BOAT

THIS novel little craft is out of the ordinary, and is very easy to build.

You will require two large round corks, although smaller ones will suffice, and if square they will do quite well. The size is immaterial, as you may make a lee-board sailing-boat of any size. A hull 12 ins. long and 3 or 4 ins. wide, however, will make an excellent craft.

A framework of wood ½ in. or less thick and about 1 in. wide will answer and should be nailed together as in the diagram. Make a bow-shaped front and nail on a block of wood about 1 in. by 1 in. by 4 ins., as shown, with a hole bored nearly through the middle to take the mast, which may be a suitable hedge-stick from which the bark has been peeled. Ash is perhaps the most suitable wood. The mast should be about the same length as the boat.

Make an ordinary leg-of-mutton or triangular sail out of thin cloth and tack to the mast. Also tack the bottom end to the boom, which is also a thin hedge-stick from which the bark has been peeled, and which should be long enough to just reach the stern of the boat.

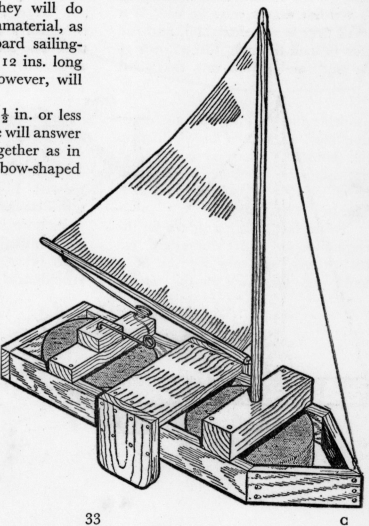

33   C

A rudder is made for the stern from wire bent into the form of a tiller at one end. After passing through a hole in a short block tacked to the stern thwart, the wire is made to fit tightly into a small piece of wood about $\frac{1}{4}$ in. thick, shaped into the form of a rudder.

A fine hole should be drilled through the rudder to take the wire (a red-hot needle may be used if a small drill is not available), and the wire pushed through, turned over at the end, and driven into the wood

again. Turning the end over in this way prevents the rudder from working loose.

A pair of lee-boards 2 ins. wide and $2\frac{1}{2}$ ins. long are tacked one to each side of the framework, and may be of thin wood or even cut from an empty tin. Give the whole a couple of coats of paint, and the boat is ready for the water. Adjust the boom by means of the "sheet", which is the length of twine for keeping the boom in position. The sheet is tied round a cleat as shown.

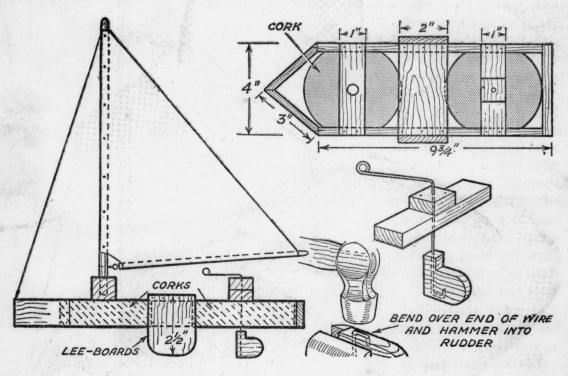

CORK

4"

3"

9¾"

CORKS

2½"

LEE-BOARDS

BEND OVER END OF WIRE AND HAMMER INTO RUDDER

BERNARD RICHARDSON

CHAPTER IX

A SIMPLE FERRYBOAT

ANOTHER very simple power boat may be made with a flat piece of wood shaped like the bottom of a flattie and powered by elastic or rubber strands. The whole craft is quite simple, but when properly made and nicely finished and painted is well worth having. It affords much fun in the running as well as pleasure in the making.

Commence with a flat piece of deal about 18 ins. long and 4 ins. wide. Saw away to form a bow and thoroughly smooth the wood with No. 1½ sandpaper.

Now construct the upper parts consisting of a deck-house about midships, about 6 ins. long, 2 ins. wide and 2 ins. high, made from thin wood tacked together and open at each end. A funnel is nailed about the middle, rising 2 ins. above the roof, and being 1 in. in diameter. A hole is bored about 3 ins. from the bow in which is tapped a mast 4 ins. high and ¼ in. thick. A series of 1-in. wire nails

35

are tapped in at regular intervals around the side of the boat about $\frac{1}{2}$ in. from the edge, to which is tied, one knot to each nail, a length of white string, to form a stanchion all round. A flag is stuck or neatly tacked to the mast-top.

This completes the top. Now for the power installation. This consists of a wedge-shaped skeg of wood 2 ins. deep and $\frac{1}{2}$ in. across at its wide end, mounted under the bow of the boat, and through which is tapped an oval nail $1\frac{1}{2}$ ins. long, leaving sufficient protruding to be bent up to form a hook. Over this hook is looped 2, 4, or 6 strands of stout rubber or elastic, to run the length of the boat, and be

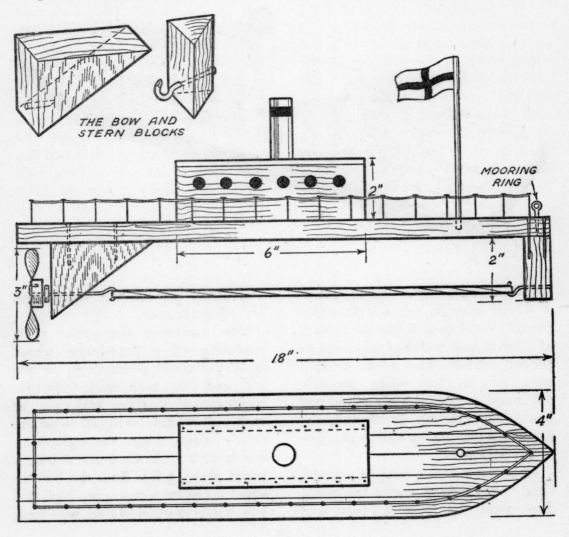

THE BOW AND STERN BLOCKS

MOORING RING

looped over the hooked end of the propeller shaft. The latter passes through a hole, in which it turns very easily, bored in another wedge-shaped block at the stern. The other end of the shaft fits tightly through a hole in a small wooden wheel about $\frac{3}{4}$ in. diameter. The wire is bent over into the wood to prevent it from slipping. To this wooden wheel the propeller is secured by tapping small pin-nails through holes made in the tinware of which the propeller is made. The two blades are cut from an empty cocoa or similar tin, 3 ins. diameter, with each blade 1 in. wide at its widest part. A washer made from a small piece of lead is used on the shaft, as a medium between propeller and wood block. Well vaseline the shaft before inserting in the hole through the block, to ensure easy run-ning. A small handle for winding may be included, as with other models described herein.

To paint the ferry-boat, use black for the funnel with a red band round the top, grey roof to the deck-house, with white for sides, and oak varnish for the deck itself, and portholes touched out in black spots along each side of the deck-house. The mast should also be white with light green for the edge of the hull's sides, also the underside and wood blocks and propeller. This gives a striking finish to a neat ferryboat that will run quite a distance. A longer run will be obtained and the rubber will last longer if thoroughly lubricated be-fore winding by one of the pre-parations specially made by firms which cater for the amateur model-maker.

CHAPTER X

A SIMPLE JET-PROPELLED BOAT

HERE is another very simple power boat that may be easily constructed, and is on the jet-propelled principle.

Make your hull as light as possible; the flattie type will suit admirably. Use ¼-in. plywood for the bottom, and thin tin will answer for the sides, or you may use thin plywood about ⅛ in. thick. See all is secured with a stout transom or sternpiece; also a bow-strengthener should be added.

The whole should be painted and tried out in water to see if there are any leaks, as these should be stopped with putty. After all is made water-tight and the paint dry, install the boiler, which should be made from an empty treacle tin or any tin that has an airtight cover. The cover should be gently tapped on after water has been placed in it. About one-third full is ample, and fresh water may be added when the amount becomes low.

The boiler is of the horizontal type and rests on a pair of stays made from strips of tin, as shown in the diagrams. Thus, it may be taken up by means of a cloth to prevent burning the hands, and fresh water placed

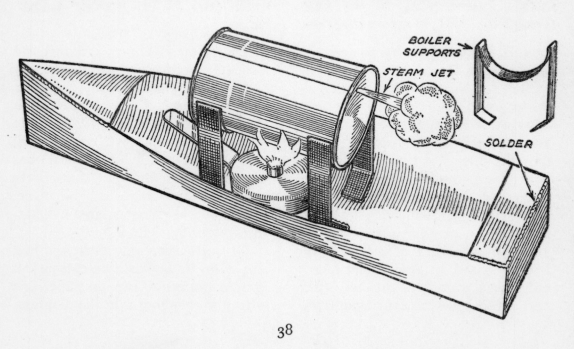

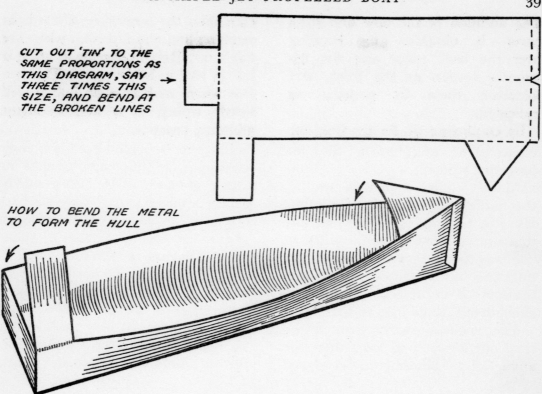

CUT OUT 'TIN' TO THE
SAME PROPORTIONS AS
THIS DIAGRAM, SAY
THREE TIMES THIS
SIZE, AND BEND AT
THE BROKEN LINES →

HOW TO BEND THE METAL
TO FORM THE HULL

in it. A small hole is made near the top for the steam to escape. The principle is similar to the simpler or earlier type of jet-propelled planes and cars. The steam, gaining pressure as the water boils, issues in force through the hole in the top of the boiler, and pressing against the air pushes or propels the boat forward. Of course this is an elementary toy boat, but affords a lot of pleasure in making and trying. Needless to say the power is quite small, so you should run it only when conditions are very calm and without any current against it.

The lamp is either a flat round vaseline tin or any similar empty tin, with a small hole made in the cover through which protrudes a wick of cotton wool. The whole inside of the lamp is filled with cotton wool, over which methylated spirit has been poured. A bow and stern cover gives a finish to the boat. The whole, too, should be nicely painted in whatever colour fancied.

Of course, you may make the hull out of tin if you wish, by cutting out from a pattern drawn on paper first after the style shown in the diagram.

The addition of the bow and stern cover is obtained by bending over the back piece and the triangular section at the front, and soldering them in position as indicated.

By employing tin for the hull one eliminates the possibility of the boat catching fire, and although with care this is not likely to happen at all, it is just as well to be prepared. This is a case where making a tin hull is well worth trying. It is also excellent soldering practice.

CHAPTER XI

A PLANK-SECTION SAILING-SHIP

THIS is rather a novel way of making a sailing-ship, requiring neither special skill nor knowledge, the idea being to cut out a series of decreasing sizes in ½-in. deal planking. It may be constructed either as a solid hull or one with the inside removed by sawing out the centre of each plank, leaving a ½ or ¾ in. or so margin of wood all round, thus producing a hollow hull. This latter, of course, entails much more work and patience, and no little care.

To construct a solid hull, which is the easier of the two, make a paper plan of size and shape of the deck and place on the planking and mark around with pencil. Then saw as marked. Cut the paper pattern about ¼ in. smaller and saw out another section and fasten to the first by thin wire nails. Repeat this procedure until the hull is the required depth. When all the sections are secured together, one has to remove the "square edge" or "corners" by aid of plane and spokeshave, thereby shaping and smoothing up the hull. Needless to say, all nails should be kept well away from the outside edges, otherwise they may come in contact with the plane or spokeshave.

A solid hull thus cut, however, makes a good sailing-ship. Start with the deck. You may make your vessel any size you wish, but 15, 18 or 21 inches are very good lengths to choose from. The width at the widest part should be about one-third of the length. Thus the above will be 5 ins., 6 ins. or 7 ins. beam or width, respectively.

About 2 ins. or so depth of hull will suffice if you are making a "solid-planking" hull, but 4 ins. deep for a "hollow" hull is more suitable. Both should have suitable keels to them. A strip of lead should be tacked or nailed along the bottom of the hull as ballast, and the weight depends on the size and depth of your ship. Better to make it too heavy than too light, as it is easy to cut away any excess weight. The mast should be about the length of the ship and is inserted in a hole bored in the deck to take it, being one-third down the length of the deck from the bow. The bowsprit may project about 3 ins. from the bow, and the boom just above the stern, with a "sheet" from a "horse" connected with it. The horse is a piece of stiff wire bent to fit snugly in a hole each side of the stern end, as shown in the diagrams, while the sheet is the twine connected from boom to horse.

If you decide to cut out the inside

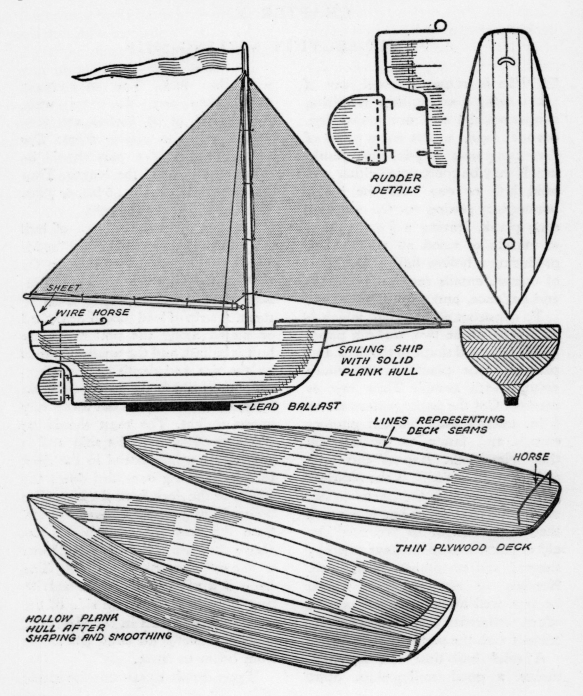

RUDDER DETAILS

SHEET

WIRE HORSE

SAILING SHIP WITH SOLID PLANK HULL

← LEAD BALLAST

LINES REPRESENTING DECK SEAMS

HORSE

THIN PLYWOOD DECK

HOLLOW PLANK HULL AFTER SHAPING AND SMOOTHING

of the hull, thus making it hollow, a deck will have to be fitted in the form of a thin piece of plywood, or any suitable wood, sawn to the same size and shape as the deck area. It is tacked down, after first forming a rim of putty around its underside edge to ensure there being no leaks between deck and hull. In fitting a mast to a hollow hull, a "step" is made by boring a hole in a small block of wood to take the end of the mast. This step is tacked to the inside bottom of the hull, right under the deck-hole, down through which the mast passes.

Use thin cloth for the sails, and these may be any colour you fancy, such as brown and red, or they may be of white material. A pennant about 3 ins. long should be secured to the mast-top. Rig your ship as shown in the diagrams. Also fit a rudder by means of two small staples in the stern end of the keel, to take the wire pivots on which the rudder turns. These pivots are two pieces of stiff wire bent as shown and driven into the wooden rudder. When the rudder is in position they hook over their respective staples. The tiller is a piece of bent wire driven into a small hole bored in the top of the rudder. A red-hot needle forms a convenient drill for boring this tiny hole. Insert the tiller after the rudder is in position and bend the end back into the wood as shown.

The tiller may be lashed to keep the rudder in the position required, or alternatively a small wooden or metal rack can be constructed with notches into which the tiller arm may be placed.

You may finish the boat in any colour you fancy, but red for keel, with jade green above to waterline, and white around from waterline to deck and mast, spars and deck oak varnished, makes a very attractive ship. Give two coats, finishing all over with clear varnish. When all is dry and hard you may try her out in a light breeze and so test her sailing qualities.

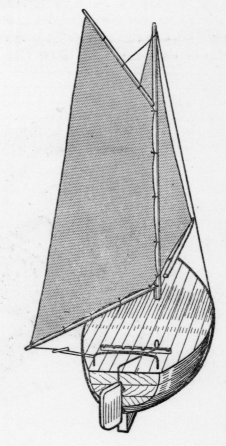

CHAPTER XII

A HYDRO GLIDER

HERE is an attractive water-craft that may easily be made, affording much fun and interest.

Use plywood if you have any, but whatever thin wood you may possess will suit quite well. Start with the floats, which should be about 10 ins. long and 1 in. square. Cut the wood neatly and secure with pin-tacks, but before tacking on the tops try each one in water and see if they leak. It is a good plan to run putty all along the joints of each float and then give a

coat of paint before immersing in water, and you will find that all is probably watertight. The lids or covers of the floats may be tacked down and the edges where the joints come be treated with putty and afterwards painted. Of course, it is essential that the floats are water-tight, and if you have any doubts it is a good plan to brush each over outside with glue and then cover neatly with muslin or thin cloth or calico, and when dry give a couple of

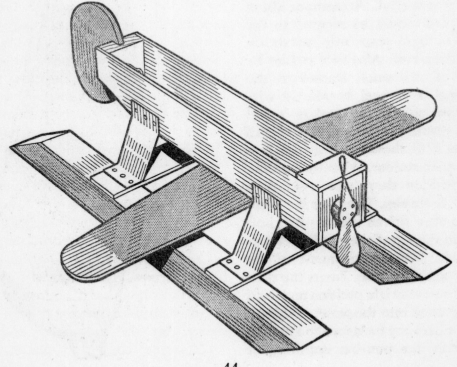

coats of copal varnish. This will ensure them both being watertight, with no fear of their future leaking. Shape the floats as shown in the diagrams.

Next make the body out of thin wood, 9 ins. long and 2 ins. square; with the wings made in one long piece 12 ins. long by 2 ins. wide, tacked to the bottom of the body about 1 in. from the front, so that it projects 5 ins. each side. You may use plywood for this or even stout cardboard, but the latter must be treated to make it impervious to water by means of paint and varnish.

The sides of the body should be shaped as shown in the diagrams, with a bow-covering and sternpiece, to which is secured a stabilizer in the form of a fin or vane 2 ins. wide and 3 ins. high. The motive power is supplied by tension rubber or elastic. Two or four strands are secured at the stern by being looped over a hook, the other end looped over the hooked end of the axle or shaft carrying the propeller. The latter is 4 ins. in diameter with two blades, and may be made of tin or thin wood secured to a small hub made of wood about $\frac{3}{4}$ in. diameter and $\frac{3}{8}$ to $\frac{1}{2}$ in. thick. The two blades must of course be given the necessary twist of about 45° to form the "pitch". Before attaching the blades, however, the wire shaft should be fitted. Bend over one end of the wire as shown and then push the wire through a tight

centre hole in the hub and drive it home by tapping it lightly with a hammer to force the turned-over end into the wood. If a small hole is pierced with a fine awl to take the turned-over point of the wire there will be less chance of splitting the wood. When the shaft is in position the other end may be bent to form a hook.

The two floats or pontoons are kept at the right distance from each other by two pieces of flat wood 1 in. wide and 6 ins. long, secured by means of panel-pins. These crosspieces are secured to the body by four uprights, each made either from stout metal or formed by bending over twice and hammering flat four pieces of tin each 3 ins. square, thus providing stout metal strips 3 ins. long and 1 in. wide, of "three-tin" thicknesses. After making four small holes at the ends of each piece with a wire nail and hammer, bend one end of each where they contact the body of the hydroglider, and also bend the other ends where they are attached by means of small screws or tacks to the floats.

This completes this excellent little craft, which may, of course, be made proportionally larger.

Give the whole a coat of paint. A good scheme consists of dark blue or French grey for the floats, with midgreen for the crosspieces and uprights, the body and plane being white with a red stabilizer and propeller. An alternative colour scheme is shown in the illustration on the cover of this book. When the paint is dry complete the job with a final coat of clear varnish.

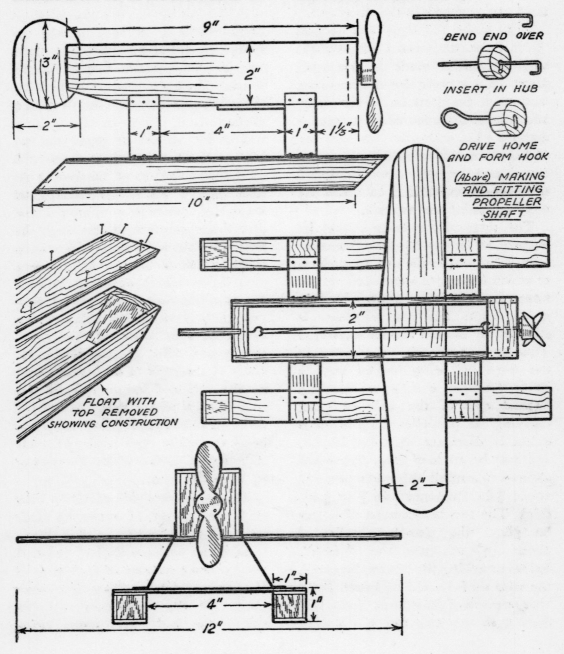

BEND END OVER

INSERT IN HUB

DRIVE HOME AND FORM HOOK

(Above) MAKING AND FITTING PROPELLER SHAFT

FLOAT WITH TOP REMOVED SHOWING CONSTRUCTION

CHAPTER XIII

A SIMPLE OUTBOARD MOTOR-BOAT

THERE are several small craft that may be very easily made, affording a lot of pleasure and enjoyment both in making and running, one being an outboard motor-boat.

Make the hull of the flattie type with thin wood bottom and the sides made of thin wood too, or you may employ Essex Board or stout waterproofed cardboard, as described in the chapter on hulls. The transom or sternpiece should be of ½-in. deal, as this has to take the outboard motor. Also a wedge-shaped strengthener should be fitted at the bow where the sides join, as the elastic has to be secured there.

You may make your hull any size in proportion, but 12 or 18 ins. long and 4 ins. wide will make an excellent outboard motor-boat. So suppose we decide to make one 18 ins. long by 4 ins. wide. Cut and shape the bottom of your hull in the usual way with sides 2½ ins. high. At the stern twin "rollers" are made from ½-in. dowelling revolving on a pivot in the form of a nail passing through holes in tin bearings pro-

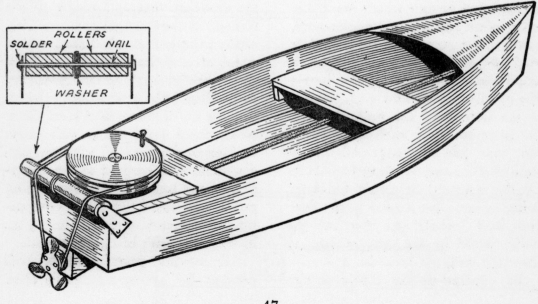

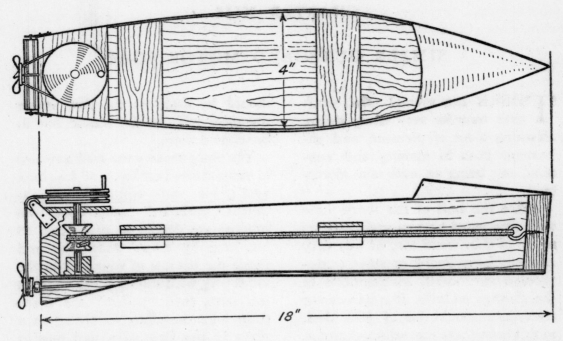

jecting from each side of the stern. (See diagrams.) A stout wooden wheel about 2 ins. in diameter and $\frac{3}{8}$ or $\frac{1}{2}$ in. thick has an axle which fits firmly in its centre and passes down through a hole in the stern-covering (which is made from plywood or any suitable wood about $\frac{1}{4}$ in. thick), and into a rest made from a cotton-reel, secured to the bottom of the hull. Between the stern-covering and the rest-reel the axle has another reel firmly secured to it, and which turns with it. On this is wound the elastic, the latter being looped over a hook at the bow end and secured to the driving pulley-wheel in the upright axle at the stern end.

By winding up the elastic on the reel, by means of a handle provided by a 1-in. wire nail gently tapped into the wooden flywheel, one obtains the necessary driving force. A groove is made in the flywheel to take a belt, made from an elastic band, which passes around the flywheel and down over the "rollers" to the propeller hub. This hub is a wooden wheel about $\frac{1}{2}$ in. diameter and $\frac{3}{8}$ in. thick, which turns easily on an axle made by hammering a $1\frac{1}{2}$-in. wire nail into a wooden skeg secured to the under-side of the hull. To this underwater pulley is tacked a two-, three- or four-bladed propeller, cut from tin $1\frac{1}{2}$ in. in diameter with blades $\frac{1}{2}$ in. wide.

All moving parts must be well greased. By having a large flywheel and a small propeller-wheel, more turns are obtained on the propeller and the boat has a longer run. For best results the rubber should be well lubricated with pure soft soap or other suitable lubricant, otherwise with this type of motor the rubber is unevenly stretched.

A bow-cover improves the appearance of the boat and you may add seats, as shown in the drawings. Give the whole a good coat of paint, using an attractive blend of colours, and you will then possess a neat little craft that will "go".

CHAPTER XIV

A SIMPLE POWER PADDLE-BOAT

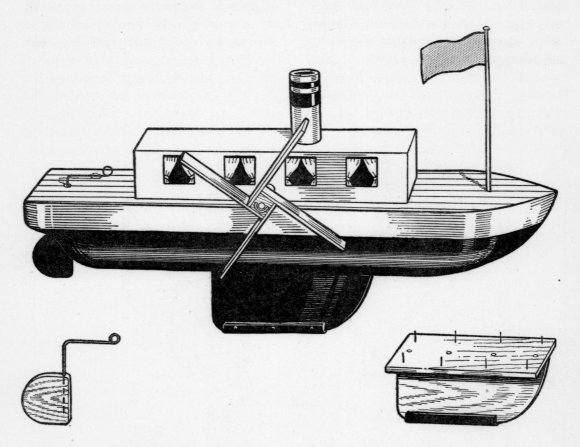

AN old-time paddle-boat is another simple and easy-to-make model, which may be made with a few ordinary tools and which is constructed almost entirely of wood. Those who are fond of woodwork will thoroughly enjoy building a model of this description.

The hull is made from a piece of 3 by 2 timber. Deal will do excellently as it is light in weight, and should be 15 ins. long. Elm, by the way, will not be suitable owing to its weight, which increases when soaked in water. Shape up as shown in the diagram, making all smooth with sandpaper. Next build your deck-housing out of fretwood, or any

kind of thin wood about $\frac{1}{8}$ in. thick
will do, making it 2 ins. wide and $1\frac{1}{2}$
ins. high and 8 ins. long. Either
paint on or cut out the port-holes
and secure the sides with panel-pins
or small tacks. A funnel is placed amid-
ships, made from a length of broom-
stick or similar piece of wood, and
should be about 2 ins. high. The
housing is secured to the deck with
screws through angle plates at the
sides, as shown in the diagram.

A mast is fitted in a hole about an
inch from the bow and $3\frac{1}{2}$ ins. high,
with a flag or pennant tacked at the
top. A keel made from a piece of
plywood, 6 ins. long and 2 ins. wide,
shaped as shown in the diagrams, is
secured to the bottom by means of
a rectangle of thin plywood, to which
it is nailed or screwed, and which in
turn is nailed to the underside of the
boat. A rudder may be fitted to the
stern by boring a hole, through
which a length of stiff wire about the
thickness of the lead of a lead pencil is

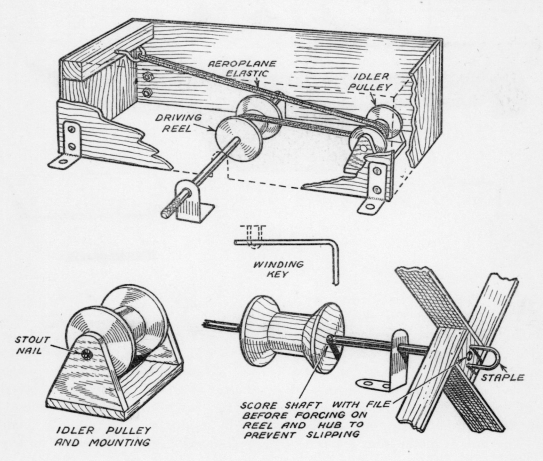

AEROPLANE ELASTIC

IDLER PULLEY

DRIVING REEL

WINDING KEY

STOUT NAIL

IDLER PULLEY AND MOUNTING

SCORE SHAFT WITH FILE BEFORE FORCING ON REEL AND HUB TO PREVENT SLIPPING

STAPLE

passed. This wire is first bent into the form of a tiller, then fed through the hole and forced into a piece of wood about $\frac{1}{4}$ in. thick and 2 ins. long and 1 in. wide, shaped like a rudder.

This completes the fittings. Now we come to the motive power and paddles. It is better to make all parts of the paddle-boat before assembling.

The paddles have eight blades in all, four each side. These are either cut from stout tin $3\frac{1}{2}$ ins. long by 1 in. wide, or from thin wood, and are tacked to a square hub 1 in. wide and 1 in. square. The axle is made from a 5-in. wire nail with its head filed off, while the bearings take the form of a pair of angle plates made by bending two pieces of stout tin, each about $\frac{3}{4}$ in. wide and $1\frac{1}{2}$ ins. long, as shown in the diagram. The angle plates are mounted opposite each other on the deck, the axle holes being about $\frac{3}{4}$ in. above the deck.

The power is supplied by means of elastic coming from the stern end of the deck-house, over an "idler" pulley at the bow end, to the reel on the paddle axle, on which it is wound by means of a key in the starboard—or right-side hub, as shown in the diagrams.

All that now remains is to paint the whole attractively.

CHAPTER XV

A YANKEE CLIPPER

"WINDJAMMER" days may be gone—but, for all we know, they may come back again. It has been stated that the finest sight in the world is a big sailing-ship under full canvas, and incidentally it might be added that in the Merchant Service of the United States there are even now, in these days of power-boats, over a thousand vessels that employ sails only as a means of progress, and carry no engines whatever.

That world-famous sailing-ship, the *Cutty Sark*, of which no doubt you have heard, was one of the China tea clippers. On one occasion she made a day run of over 350 miles. This was during one of the "Annual Grain Races" which each year draw nearly all the square-rigged sailing-ships in the world to the

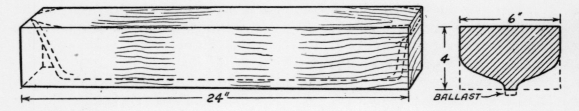

wheat-loading ports of South Australia, there to load up with wheat and then enter for the competitive run to Falmouth.

By the way, many and strange are the superstitions regarding sailing-ships. A feminine figurehead is considered lucky; yet to give a wind-jammer a feminine name is considered unlucky! To whistle while at work on board a sailing-ship is very wrong, yet to sing is quite in order. Whistling is supposed to cause high winds and gusty squalls.

Suppose we try our hand at making a model after the style of one of these famous clippers.

Commence with the hull, which should be about four times the length of its width. That is to say, if you choose to make one 24 ins. long, it should be about 6 ins. wide at its widest part, and the depth of the hull about 4 ins. As these dimensions are not to scale, a rough estimate will suffice, for to make a clipper exactly to scale with everything in proportion would entail skill and ability of a very high order, as well as much time and patience and some extra tools. We can, however, make a fair model which will give pleasure both in building and sailing.

Suppose we make one 24 ins. long and 6 ins. wide. All the clippers had sharp bows to shear their way through the water, and you may make your hull from a block of suitable wood such as pine or deal. It should be about 4 ins. deep. You may be able to obtain a piece of deal 24 ins. by 6 ins. by 4 ins. thick from a timber merchant, or a local builder might saw off a piece for you from an old gate-post or beam.

Alternatively you may build your hull of plank-sections as described in the chapter on hulls. If you have a vice to hold your hull while carving, this is a great advantage, otherwise one must work against a "bench-stop", shaping each side carefully until all is symmetrical.

If you want to make a big job of it, then hollow out the inside of the block of wood so as to make your hull as light as possible. Of course, a hollow hull makes a better ship than a solid one, but it entails considerable time and care. You will require chisels and gouges such as are used for woodcarving.

A fair ship may be made from a block nicely shaped up. The whole should be smoothed over well with sandpaper. Test her floating capabilities and see she rides the water on an even keel. If a bit lop-sided, carve slightly to reduce the leaning over, until she floats quite level. See Chapter III regarding manner of doing this.

Next bore your holes for the masts. A clipper sometimes had four, counting in the smaller one near the stern, but three masts should suffice for our clipper. The mainmast stands about the centre of the hull, with the

ins. high from the deck to top, and the other two about 9 ins. The bowsprit should jut out about 3 ins. over the bow.

Although the clippers had six sails to the mainmast, three will suffice for ours, with bottom cross-trees about 8 ins. wide, and decreasing about 2 ins. in width for each successive cross-tree above. Fitting the sails requires care and patience, and if you make your sails to be raised and lowered this will also entail extra fitting, time and work. Therefore if you sail the little vessel only when there is a moderate breeze you may dispense

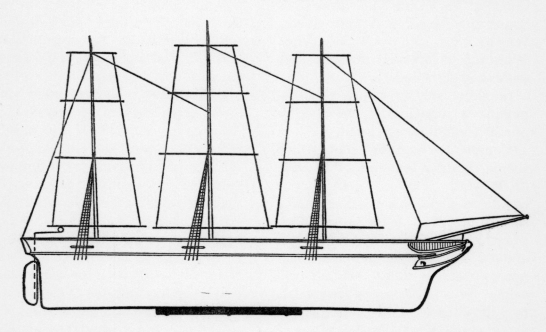

foremast 6 ins. to the fore of it and the mizzenmast, or rear mast, 6 ins. to the stern of it.

The mainmast should be about 12

with the extra rigging and lightly tack the sails to the cross-trees. Of course, in a full-size ship, when the wind is too strong, the sails are reefed down.

However, complete your rigging with pennants to each of the masts. Imitation "rope" ladders or "ratlines" made from twine, thin fishing-line or Strutt's Macrame twine, greatly add to the ship's appearance.

It may be necessary to nail or tack a strip of lead along the bottom of the keel in order to ballast the ship, otherwise you may find the craft has a tendency to capsize in a stiff breeze.

A rudder is made by passing a stout piece of wire through a hole in the stern and then inserting it into a hole bored down into the rudder-top.

The wire should fit tightly into the rudder.

As regards painting, red below the waterline and white above, with deck and spars in oak varnish, looks well.

And while building and sailing your clipper, to sing a song taken from an old-time shanty would be quite in keeping with the tradition of the sea. No doubt many of you know the following opening verse:

Down the river hauled a Yankee clipper,
And it's blow, my bully boys, blow!
She'd a Yankee mate and a Yankee
*   skipper,*
And it's blow, my bully boys, blow!

CHAPTER XVI

A MODEL POWER WARSHIP

HERE is another very simple yet strikingly attractive model to make.

Commence with the hull, which in this case is a flat piece of light wood, like deal or packing-case wood, about $\frac{1}{2}$ in. or more thick, 18 ins. long and 4 ins. wide. Shape up by sawing away the bow and rounding off the stern. Then nail a wedge-shaped bow-piece as shown, and in this screw a small eye-screw. At the stern is mounted a similar wedge, through which is drilled a hole to take the propeller shaft. This consists of a length of stout wire, the inside end being bent into a closed hook and the outside end tapped through the centre of a small disc of wood. It should fit very tightly and pass through sufficiently

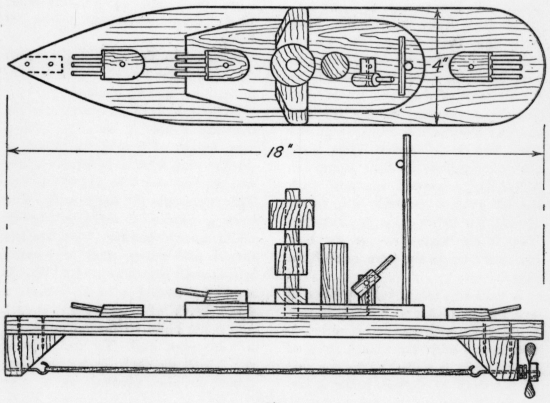

to be bent back into the form of a small "U", the short arm of the "U" being driven into the wooden disc.

The propeller is cut from an empty tin and is 4 ins. in diameter, having two blades, which must be slightly twisted to give the necessary thrust when revolving. These are secured to the inside of the wooden disc. For the motive power, four or six strands of rubber about $\frac{1}{8}$ in. wide will be required, and are stretched from bow eye-screw to propeller-hook. If thin rubber strands are used, you may require more.

You can now complete the top side of the hull. This consists of "built-up" parts, with three gun-turrets, each possessing three guns, the turrets being made of wood blocks $1\frac{1}{2}$ ins. long and 1 in. wide. Drill three holes for insertion of the guns, made from dowels or wooden skewers or even suitable hedge-sticks from which the bark has been peeled. The guns should fit tightly in their respective holes, being tapped in, and each should project beyond the turret about 1 in., being $\frac{3}{16}$ in. in diameter. Two of the turrets are at the bow end and one at the stern end of the ship.

A deck-top made from a piece of wood 1 in. thick and 8 ins. long and 3 ins. wide, with one end rounded to correspond with the round stern of the warship, is nailed to the top side of the deck as shown, being 4 ins.

from the stern. Just behind the forward second gun-turret, and about $9\frac{1}{2}$ ins. from the bow, comes the "fighting-top", which is made from a $4\frac{1}{2}$ in. length of $\frac{1}{2}$ in. dowel or similar round stick, and tapped into a hole bored in the deck. Over this is slipped a piece of $\frac{1}{2}$-in. thick deal 4 ins. long and 1 in. wide, tapering at the ends as shown. Half an inch above this unit is a similar one, only being 1 in. shorter and $\frac{1}{2}$ in. thicker, making it 3 ins. long by 1 in. thick. This, too, is shaped as shown in the diagrams. About $\frac{1}{2}$ in. above this is another unit 1 in. thick and $1\frac{1}{2}$ ins. diameter, made from a round piece of wood.

About 1 in. farther along towards the stern is the funnel, which is 1 in. in diameter and $2\frac{1}{2}$ ins. high.

At the middle of the stern end of the deck-top a hole is bored to take a 6-in. length of $\frac{1}{4}$ or $\frac{3}{8}$ in. dowel or similar stick with a crosspiece 2 ins. wide tacked to it 1 in. below the top. This represents the aerial mast. The stern gun-turret is fitted as shown, while about midway between the funnel and aerial mast a dummy anti-aircraft gun is mounted. This is made by boring a hole through a small block of wood $\frac{1}{2}$ in. square and 1 in. high, so that it pivots on a 1-in. wire nail. To the side of the block an inch length of $\frac{1}{2}$-in. dowel is also pivoted by a wire nail. Into a hole in the centre of the dowel is tapped a 1-in. piece of round wood $\frac{1}{8}$ in. in diameter.

This completes the top fittings, which give the craft a realistic effect without overcrowding the top.

Appropriate painting gives the warship its finishing touches and includes giving it first of all a couple of coats of grey paint, to be followed when dry by black round the funnel top. Port-holes are picked out with dots of black paint. Use yellow round the gun-mouths with a black dot in the centre of each gun-end to represent the hollow gun-bore. A final coat of clear varnish completes this striking and attractive model.

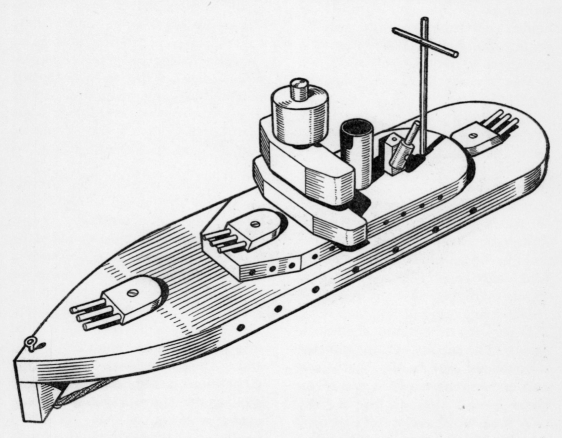

CHAPTER XVII

A MODEL OLD-TIME GALLEON

A FAIR model of an old-time galleon may easily be made with a little care and application. Use softwood such as deal for the hull. First of all make the keel, and this should be about ¼ in. thick—the exact dimensions of your galleon do not matter, but should be in proportion.

Supposing you decide to make your galleon 18 ins. long and 4 ins. wide or beam, then the rest should be in keeping with this length and breadth. Cut the keel with a padsaw, making it 18 ins. long by 4 ins. wide, shaping up as in the diagrams, and nail on each side a quartern cut from a piece of round wood 4 ins. in diameter. This gives you a hull 2 ins. deep, with the keel also 2 ins. deep in the centre.

BERNARD RICHARDSON

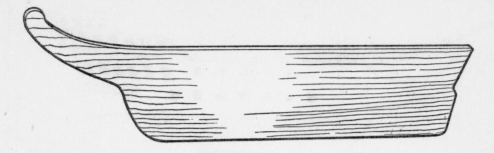

If you haven't a suitable piece of round wood you may employ a square piece. Place it in the vice, using a piece of odd thin wood on either side to protect the work from being damaged by the vice jaws. Then, with a draw-knife or spokeshave and small plane, shape up the hull into the required contour. Care and application is necessary to ensure making a neat and satisfactory job of it. When

completed, immerse in water to ascertain that the hull floats level.

If it leans to one side, pare a little at a time off the opposite side until the whole floats on an even keel. See also Chapter III regarding this point.

The waterline should be marked and then a piece of sheet lead bent to fit along the keel a few inches each side of the centre. Just how much

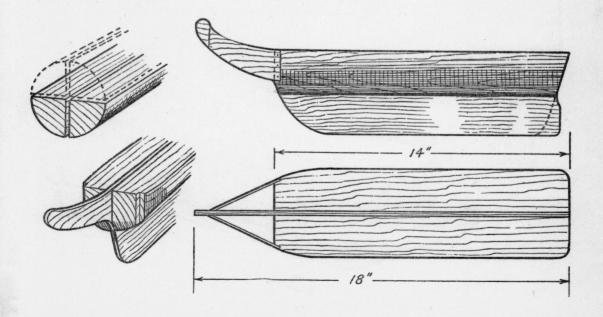

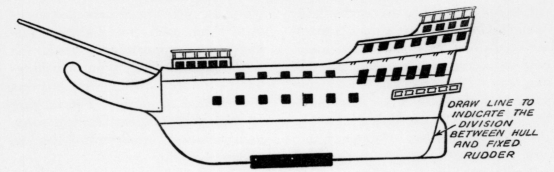

DRAW LINE TO
INDICATE THE
DIVISION
BETWEEN HULL
AND FIXED
RUDDER

lead is necessary can best be found by first "pinching" on the keel a generous piece of lead, and if too heavy, causing the hull to sink too low in the water, removing a little at a time until you obtain the desired effect.

Having got all this completed, next

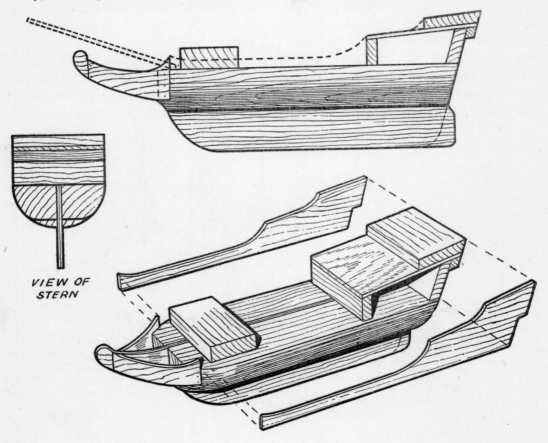

VIEW OF
STERN

cut blocks of wood to fit on the deck in accordance with the architecture of the old-time galleons. This may best be ascertained by studying the diagrams. These blocks, after being shaped and smoothed, are nailed on to the deck. Use sandpaper No. 1½, to be followed by No. o to smooth the hull, deck and fittings.

Next see to the masts. ½-in. dowel for the two main masts will do excellently, with ¼ in. or so for the two smaller ones. Your "mast-tops" as shown in the diagrams may be made from a bisected cotton-reel or spool, as these make first-class mast-tops. From each one of these, "rat-lines" or rope-ladders should be fastened, made from twine or fishing-line. Thin brown fishing-line answers the purpose admirably. The making of these rope-ladders requires some patience and application. Rig as shown.

Next fit the bowsprit. A figurehead made from plastic wood may be fitted over the bow, and will greatly improve the galleon's appearance. Cross-trees are made of thin round wood, such as thin wooden skewers or

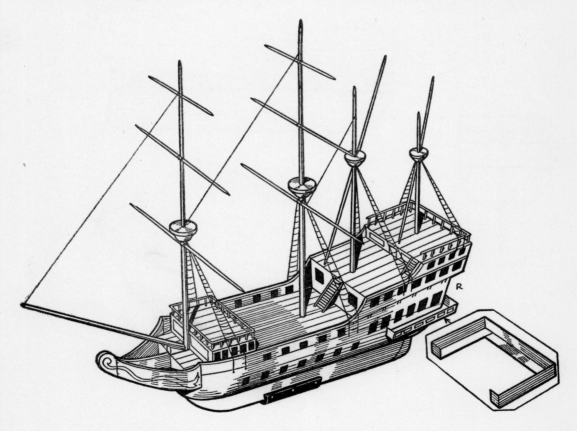

thin dowels. The sails are made of calico or any suitable thin material. Shape and cut out as shown and finish the edges with a neat hem.

If you paint the hull below the waterline venetian red with white sides and a blue line round the top, and oak varnish the deck, masts and spars, it will give the whole a striking finish. The figurehead should, of course, be painted in appropriate colours. When all is dry, a coat of clear varnish will lend a glossy finish to your galleon, and you will then possess a striking and attractive model. Days when a light breeze is blowing are the more suitable for sailing this vessel.

CHAPTER XVIII

A ROTOR SHIP

HERE is something quite unusual in ships, which no doubt will appeal more especially to those interested in anything very modern or scientific.

This type of craft is more or less in experimental stages among ship-building firms, although the Germans built a successful vessel on the rotor principle called the *Buckau* before the last war.

Unlike the old-type sailing-ships, which were propelled mainly by the pressure of the wind against the sails, a rotor ship has revolving vanes or pillars, which cause a partial vacuum in much the same way as an aeroplane propeller or wing operates. One might call a rotor ship a cross between sailing and flying.

The making of a simple little rotor sailer will give a lot of fun, and if you are fond of experimenting you may learn a lot about wind currents and pressure of the air, besides gaining a practical insight into the rudiments of the idea of this novel type of craft. After having made a simple model of No. 1 type, we'll try our hands at a more elaborate model.

In the first instance a start might be made with a very simple model. Nothing is bound to scale and the dimensions given are not hard and fast. The materials and tools are of the simplest and the cost practically negligible.

Start with the hull. The flattie type will do quite well, making it about 12 ins. long, 3 ins. wide, with sides about $2\frac{1}{2}$ ins. deep, after the style already described in the chapter on hulls. Use wood, cardboard or calico. A keel about 1 in. deep, made from a piece of plywood $\frac{1}{4}$ in. thick and shaped as shown in the diagrams, may be attached to the bottom to steady the boat.

In this model the rotor vane revolves by action of the wind, while the mast is stationary. The latter, which is made from dowel rod, is about 12 ins. long and passes through a hole in the crosspiece and down into a hole in a rest-stay, secured to the bottom of the boat directly under the crosspiece. On this mast is dropped the rotor vane, on which it revolves freely. The rotor is made of oval-shaped wood supports covered with light cardboard or calico, afterwards well varnished with copal varnish. The lower oval-shaped support is 3 ins. wide and made from plywood or any thin wood, the support half-way up the mast being 2 ins.

wide and the top one 1 in., each with a hole in its centre to turn easily on the mast. Thus we have a tapering vane that slips over the mast and on which it turns freely. Thin slips of wood or strips of stout cardboard should be secured to the ovals longways to keep them in their place and at the right distance apart, before covering with cardboard or calico. The three oval-shaped discs should be narrow, the bottom one being 3 ins. by 1 in., the next 2 ins. by $\frac{3}{4}$ in., and the top one 1 in. by $\frac{1}{2}$ in. A washer should be placed on the mast before slipping over the vane, and some grease or vaseline also applied to ensure easy turning.

Choose a suitable day with a nice breeze blowing, and place your rotor sail-craft in pond, lake, river, pool or harbour and the wind will rotate the vane, causing the little ship to forge onward.

There was a rotor ship that attracted much attention among yachtsmen a few years ago in which the rotors were made to revolve by means of an engine. The rotors in this case were circular and not oval, for it was discovered that circular or cylindrical rotors upon being revolved caused "suction" and "pressure zones". Thus the vessel would travel in calm weather and not have to depend on the wind. The rotors being made to revolve caused the vacuum, and the resulting air pressure drove the ship along. A Finnish sailor invented S-shaped rotor vanes, the advantages of which were doubtful.

However, having given our freevane rotor ship a try-out, we'll next make a mechanically-operated rotor ship with the circular rotors made to revolve independently of the wind, so that it may be sailed in calm weather—quite the reverse of the usual sailing craft which needs wind to provide the motive power. One might argue that the power employed to drive the rotors might well be used to turn a propeller. But those who have experimented state that far more power would be necessary to drive the vessel forward at similar speed by means of a propeller or propellers than the power required to drive the rotors. This can be understood, as there is comparatively little resistance to the rotors revolving, whereas a propeller in the water requires considerable power to turn it, according to the size of the propeller and weight of the ship. Of course, as already stated, this type of ship is still in the experimental stage. There is, however, a delightful fascination about experimenting.

You might like this time to construct a power rotor ship employing three rotors, with a hull say 24 ins. long by 6 ins. wide, with sides 3 ins. high.

Assemble the crosspieces that are to take the three rotor pillars first. These should have about 6 ins.

space between each with rest-block sockets directly under, to take the uprights or rotor pillar masts. The rest-blocks are made from small blocks of wood about 1 in. square, with a hole about ¾ in. deep in which the mast rests. A washer should be dropped over each mast before placing on the rotors, to ensure easy running.

stand about 12 ins. above the cross-pieces, their full length being 15 ins.

To each of the bottom discs of the rotors is tacked the pulleys, bobbins, or cotton-reels. And it is a good plan to saw your cotton-reels in half, tacking to the disc so that the "flange" end is below. This with the disc forms a

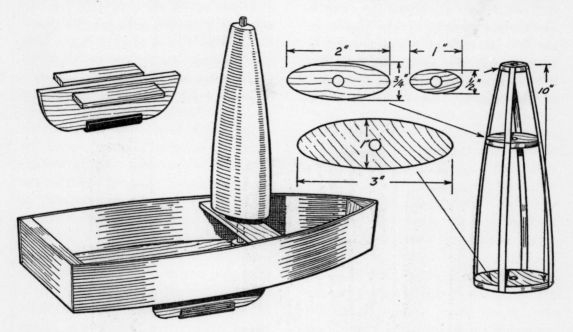

ning. The cotton-reels or pulleys of each mast are coupled together by means of belts made from hat elastic or rubber bands. The bow rotor also has a reel on which the elastic or rubber strand is wound to supply the power.

To make the rotors, cut out in thin wood nine discs 3 ins. in diameter, being three to each mast. The masts

satisfactory pulley, as shown in the diagrams.

Do not have your belts too tight, but just enough to turn each rotor easily, otherwise they will drag rather than help; moreover, there will be a strain on the structure and mechanism. The power rotor has three pulleys, made by employing three half-reels, two being below the thwart and one above. All three, however, must fit tightly on the dowel mast, so that they all revolve in unison. The upper one is the power-belt pulley, the next below being the driving one to which is attached the driving elastic or rubber strand, while the bottom pulley has some fine twine wound round it with a small ring at the end. Pulling out the string causes the rotor to revolve and winds up the elastic on the second pulley. A catch may be fitted at the bow as shown. One has only to release the catch and the pull of the elastic causes the rotor to revolve, its power being conveyed to the two other rotors by means of the belts, while the twine automatically winds up again ready for another winding. Make sure, however, that the twine is free to be drawn back round the pulley again as the rotors revolve; also that the pulleys move freely and easily.

If you study the diagrams you will see just how to construct the power unit. The rotors should have very thin cardboard tacked to their wooden discs, after which give the whole a coat of copal varnish, or shellac will

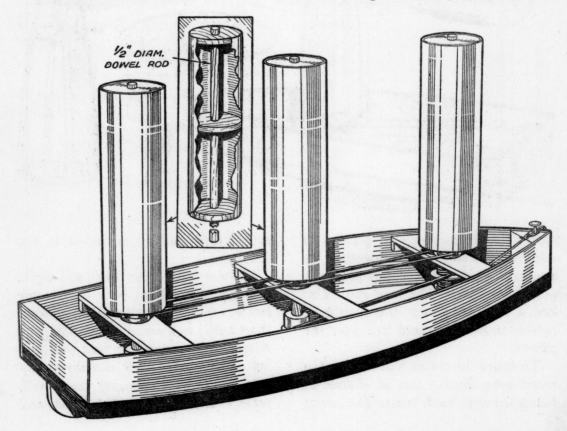

½" DIAM. DOWEL ROD

do instead. This will protect the cardboard from moisture. A finishing coat of either bronze or aluminium paint will greatly enhance their appearance.

The hull may be painted any colour desired, but blue with aluminium colour rotors looks very attractive. An alternative colouring is blue hull and green rotors. Inside the vessel you may use grey or white.

All moving parts should be well coated with vaseline or grease, and the rubber with soft soap. Wind it up and set your model on the water where it has room to move without knocking into something, choosing a calm spot, and watch the result.

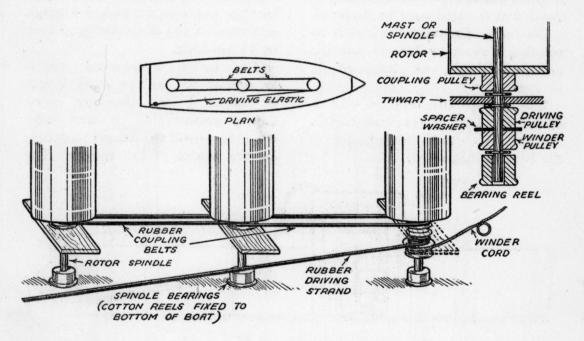

CHAPTER XIX

A STEAM TURBINE BOAT

THE hull is our first consideration, and there are several ways in which we can make it. As, however, it requires a spirit-lamp on board to heat the water, it will be readily understood that the hull must be fireproof.

One way of making the hull is by bending a sheet of thin tin into the necessary shape, as described in Chapter II.

But perhaps the simplest way to make the hull is to construct a "flattie" by cutting out the bottom of the boat in thin wood.

You may make your craft any size you wish, but 15 ins. by 4 ins. wide is a convenient one. Tack a lining of thin tin on the bottom of the boat to make the wood fireproof. The sides, too, are made of tin tacked around, as shown in the diagrams, and may be 2½ ins. high.

The boiler is a small treacle or similar tin with a short length of about $\frac{1}{16}$ in. diameter metal tubing soldered to it and bent round to permit the steam to impinge on the blades of the turbine. The

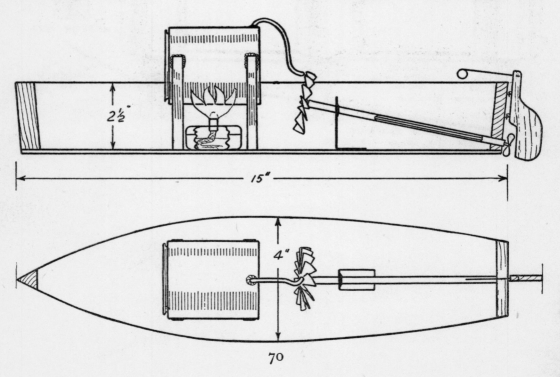

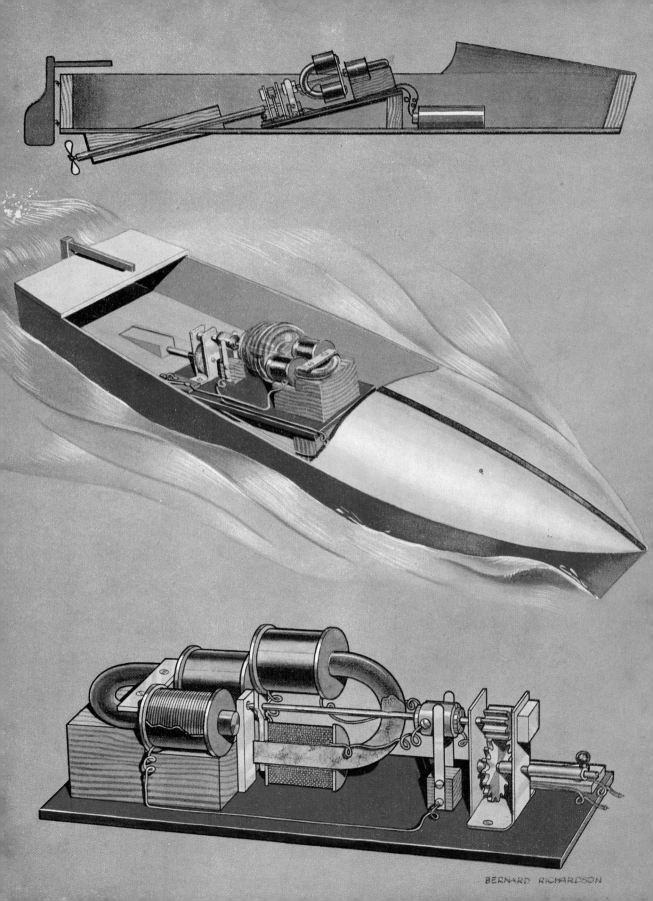

BERNARD RICHARDSON

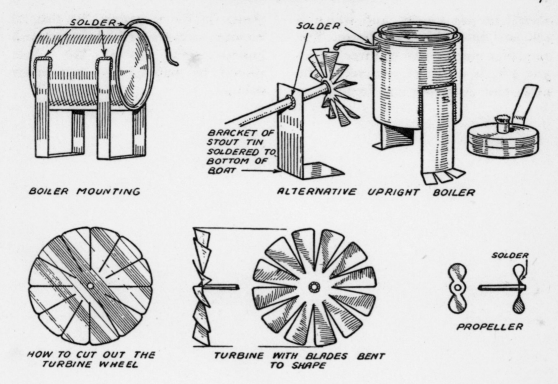

BOILER MOUNTING

ALTERNATIVE UPRIGHT BOILER

HOW TO CUT OUT THE TURBINE WHEEL

TURBINE WITH BLADES BENT TO SHAPE

PROPELLER

spirit-lamp may be a discarded ink-bottle. One of the dwarf or "squatty" type is best, as it must not be high, or the boiler will have to be higher up to be above it, and this will not improve the balance or centre of gravity of the boat. Actually a flat tin for your lamp would be the more suitable. Cottonwool soaked with methylated spirit is the best form of fire-box. The boiler should not be more than about one-third full of water, and the airtight lid just gently tapped on with the finger, so that it may act as a safety-valve by blowing off or lifting up should the steam press too hard.

The turbine is made from a circle of tin about 2 ins. in diameter, such as the cover of a tin from which the overlap edges have been cut. About 12 blades are made by making twelve cuts towards the centre and then each blade given a slight twist to about 45°; also if each blade is bent to make it slightly concave it is an advantage. The turbine vanes are then soldered to a shaft made from any straight piece of wire about $\frac{1}{8}$ in. thick. The shaft passes through a piece of metal tubing, in which it should fit just loosely, and which is soldered in position as shown. The propeller may be two or three blades and $\frac{3}{4}$ in. in diameter, soldered to the other end. A rudder may be fitted as shown in the diagrams. See that all moving parts are well lubricated with either vaseline or oil. The whole should be painted in appropriate colours.

CHAPTER XX

AN ELECTRIC LAUNCH

THERE is something fascinating about an electric launch, particularly to those interested in electricity.

The hull comes first, and this may be of the "flattie" type, as these are the more simple and easy to make. Use $\frac{3}{16}$ or $\frac{1}{4}$ in. plywood for the bottom, and carefully cut to shape. Next make the sides and sternpiece, as shown in the diagrams, in which the measurements are given. Use No. 1½

or bath of water and see how she takes it. The hull should lie evenly on the water and float gracefully, also there must be no leaks. Should any occur, these should be attended to.

Now fit the brass or copper stern-tube. The diameter of this will naturally depend on the size of the propeller-shaft, which should be an easy-running fit in the tube. Bore a clean small hole about 8 ins. from the

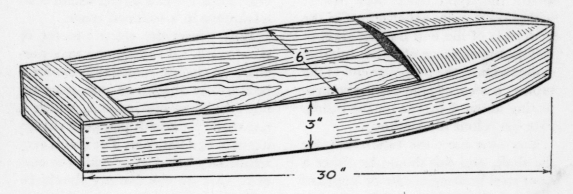

sandpaper, and finish with No. o. If you use too coarse sandpaper it will scratch rather than smooth up the wood. After you have completed the hull, give the whole a good coat of paint, and if you have doubts about it being watertight, work in a layer of putty along the joints. After all is dry give the hull a good try-out in a tub

stern in the bottom of the hull and insert the tube, which should fit tightly. Making a hole in the bottom of a boat and fitting a stern-tube always requires care and patience. Perhaps the better way is temporarily to secure the bottom of the boat to a thick piece of odd wood and then drill through the hull bottom, keeping the drill on an incline to correspond with the required slope of the tube and shaft.

Another method is to make red-hot a wire nail or length of iron rod of the right thickness to correspond with the tube's diameter, and burn a hole through. Hold the nail at the right angle by aid of a good pair of pliers or pincers, or in a small hand-clamp.

A small wedge-shaped block of wood on the inside of the hull is nailed or screwed to the bottom, with the tube passing through it and projecting about ¼ in. If you put putty around the hole where the tube passes through the bottom, and then secure the wood block over this, it will make it quite watertight. On the underside of the hull bottom another wedge-shaped piece of wood, suitably drilled to take the propeller end of the tubing, is secured; the latter also projecting about ¼ in., as on the inside. (See the colour illustration.)

You now have the tube ready for the shaft, and this should be either a stout steel knitting-needle or length of steel rod. But any length of stout wire, or brass or copper rod, will answer quite well, providing it is quite straight. At one end solder the propeller, which may be made from stout brass, copper, or even tin or iron. If the latter, give a good coat of aluminium paint to prevent corroding; or, of course, one may purchase a ready-made brass propeller. It should have three

blades and be 2 ins. in diameter. This shaft is then well vaselined or greased and inserted in the tube. The top end is to take the reduction gear.

About one-third down the length of the boat comes the hood, canopy or cover, with speed-line painted down its centre. This may be made of tin, or whatever suitable metal you happen to possess. But thin plywood will answer quite well, or even stout cardboard, if treated with sealing-wax or glue as already given previously in the chapter on making hulls.

You may fit a rudder, and by keeping it half-way to starboard or port—that is, right or left—cause the craft to career in a circle, which is an advantage in a confined space.

Now comes the electric motor or power unit. Of course, one may purchase an electric motor suitable for a boat ready made, or one may try one's hand at making one, which is not really a difficult job, only requiring care and patience. The cost is very small. Dry batteries provide the current. One 4½-volt battery should be sufficient to run the motor, but two would give more power. If more than one is used, they should be connected in series. That is to say, the positive of one battery should be connected to the negative of the next. A switch, too, is fitted, as shown. This is to cut off the current any time you wish, and so stop the motor.

As we are making an electric

launch we will try our hands at making the power unit ourselves. If you study the publications or periodicals that deal in electrical goods you will probably see small motor castings for sale, the firms also supplying the wire and parts ready to put together. But perhaps the better plan is to tell you how to make a simple motor yourself. If you want to simplify the making, the best way is to get the assistance of your local garage or ironmonger to drill holes through the iron as required.

You will require two magnets made of soft round iron $\frac{3}{8}$ in. in diameter and $5\frac{1}{2}$ ins. long. These must each be bent into the form of a horseshoe, both being the same width apart at the poles. One magnet is stationary and the other has a $\frac{1}{8}$-in. hole drilled through the centre of its bend through which is passed an axle, as shown in the diagrams. The best way is, perhaps, to get a blacksmith, or machine-shop or even a garage, to supply these two magnets, one with a hole drilled as stated. It would be a matter of only a few pence inclusive. Or, failing your being able to obtain the magnets locally, an electrical supply firm would provide them for a small charge. All the other parts you can make yourself.

Having obtained the magnets, they must next be made "soft". To do this, leave them in the fire overnight, so that they first become red-hot and afterwards cool slowly. The softening process is simply one whereby the iron is first heated to red heat and then allowed to cool very slowly, and may be accomplished by any method available. Having made them "soft", next clean them up with file and emery paper, seeing that the poles are filed smooth and even.

The "still" magnet is called the "field magnet", and the one that has the axle the "armature". This latter revolves at high speed. The first thing is to wind the field magnet with insulated copper wire. The wire has to be purchased from an electrical supply firm. Ask for No. 28 S.C.C. (single cotton covered). Next make two "bobbins", each 1 in. long, to fit over the poles of the magnet, by cutting out four discs in stout cardboard about 1 in. in diameter, and joining them together in pairs with paper tubes made by winding stiff paper around the magnets. On these bobbins the wire is wound; and, strange as it may sound, the wire must be wound round the magnet yet be insulated from it. If it were not the current would be short-circuited and the iron would not be magnetized.

To wind the magnet correctly—and this is important—place the two bobbins on the poles, with about $\frac{1}{4}$ in. iron protruding (see diagrams), and give them both a coat of shellac varnish. Shellac varnish is made by

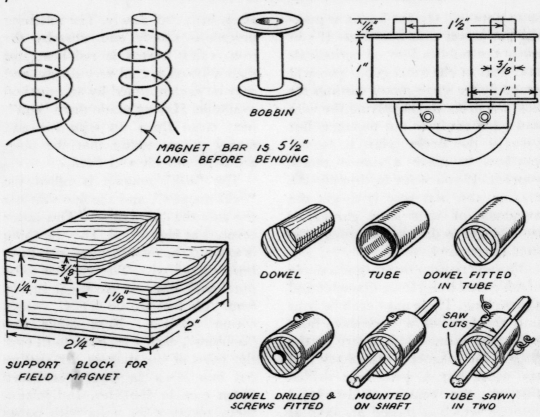

BOBBIN

MAGNET BAR IS 5½" LONG BEFORE BENDING

SUPPORT BLOCK FOR FIELD MAGNET

DOWEL   TUBE   DOWEL FITTED IN TUBE

DOWEL DRILLED & SCREWS FITTED   MOUNTED ON SHAFT   SAW CUTS   TUBE SAWN IN TWO

MAKING THE COMMUTATOR

obtaining shellac from a chemist or colour merchant—about ½ oz. or less will be ample—and dissolving it in methylated spirit. Place in a wide-necked bottle and cover the shellac with the spirit. Both the spirit and the shellac are cheap to buy. Leave for a while until all is dissolved. If too thick, add more spirit. Paint both the bobbins with a small brush, and when dry give another coat. Keep your "shellac varnish" well corked or the contents will evaporate.

About 4 ozs. of the No. 28 S.C.C. wire will be enough. Leave about 6 ins. or more of wire free, and begin to wind like the hands of a clock, beginning at the "bend" end of the bobbin and wind very carefully and evenly up and down the bobbin, keeping the coils tight so that they lie snug and even. Wind 1 oz. up and down on the bobbin. Then cross over to the other pole at the "bend" end of the bobbin, passing the wire under the magnet-pole, and wind on up and down until an ounce is also wound on this pole. As nearly as possible the same number of layers or coils and the same amount of wire should be wound on each pole. If you stop between each coil and give the layer a coat of the shellac varnish and allow to dry, a first-class job will result, both as regards insulation and in keeping the coils evenly and neatly wound. Shellac varnish dries as a hard, smooth surface, thereby providing an excellent surface to wind the next layer on. There is no fear of the coils slipping when varnished. Both these magnets are wound in this way and both have their connections at the "bend" end of the magnet. (See diagrams.)

Before winding the armature magnet—that is, the one which revolves—fix the axle. This should be either a suitably long wire nail, with the head filed off, or a length of steel rod or a knitting-needle. This should be long enough to project about $\frac{1}{4}$ in. beyond the poles end of the magnet, to which it should be soldered, and extend about 2 ins. the other end.

File or grind both ends of the axle to a "point" and make a bearing for the axle to run in, as shown.

Next it is best to make the "commutator", without which the motor would not function. The whole reason for the commutator is automatically to "switch off" the current just at the moment when the two magnet poles, by reason of their magnetic attraction, are exactly opposite one another.

If it were not for the commutator automatically switching off the current, or breaking the circuit, the armature would stop in that position, with the poles facing one another. However, the commutator cuts off the current automatically in the course of its revolving. Thus the magnets are both "dead", and the swing of the armature on its axle carries it with its poles past the stationary magnet-poles. But the instant it is past the current is automatically "switched" on again, but in the *reverse* direction. Each armature pole does not, however, swing back to the fixed pole because, owing to the reversal of current, the moving pole is now *repelled* by the fixed pole which it has just passed. It is thus helped on its way through 180° to a position opposite the other fixed pole to which it is being *attracted*. Having reached this position the current is again cut off and reversed by the commutator, and so the armature moves round once more. This action is repeated, and continues as long as the batteries supply the necessary current.

The commutator is merely a piece of brass tube about $\frac{1}{2}$ in. long and $\frac{1}{2}$ in. diameter, mounted on a similar section of wood dowel that is slightly pared to fit tightly in the brass tube. A hole is drilled through the centre of the dowel to permit the axle to fit tightly. A hole is bored through the brass tube into the wood, one on each side and exactly opposite one another, and a small brass screw is screwed into the wood, securing the brass to the wood. Note that the screws must not be long enough to go through to the axle, otherwise a short circuit will occur. The ends from the armature-magnet coils are bared of their cotton covering and one wire from each of the two bobbins on the poles is passed round each screw, which is then screwed tight. But before connecting up, the brass tube is filed in half on both sides, as shown in the diagrams. Thus the two halves are kept on the wood dowel by the screw, with the filed gaps exactly opposite one another.

Each gap must be in line with one of the armature magnet-poles. Two "brushes" made of thin springy brass or copper gauze are mounted one on either side of the commutator and connected as shown. Thus the "gap" or break in the armature current occurs just as the two magnets' poles are opposite one another. All this is very easily understood by studying the diagrams.

Outside the bearing end of the axle is the "gearwheel", which may be a small one taken from an old clock, although these gearwheels may be purchased quite cheaply. But if you select one from a discarded clock, the pinion wheel is the better wheel and must be firmly secured on the shaft,

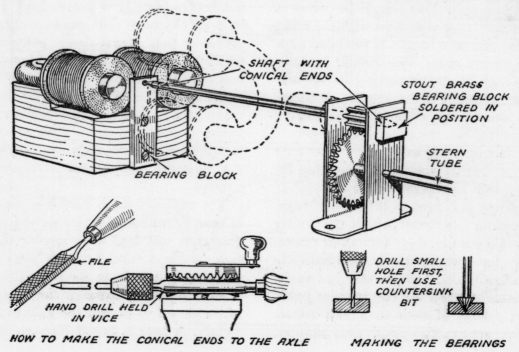

SHAFT WITH CONICAL ENDS

STOUT BRASS BEARING BLOCK SOLDERED IN POSITION

STERN TUBE

BEARING BLOCK

FILE

HAND DRILL HELD IN VICE

HOW TO MAKE THE CONICAL ENDS TO THE AXLE

DRILL SMALL HOLE FIRST, THEN USE COUNTERSINK BIT

MAKING THE BEARINGS

and unless it fits tightly must be soldered on. The pointed end of the shaft should then rest in a hole bored into a piece of stout brass, which forms the end bearing. The other pointed end of the shaft rests also in a similar stout brass bearing secured to the wooden field-magnet block. (See diagrams.)

The pinion wheel must drive a larger wheel about 1 in. in diameter, which runs freely on bearings with its axle extending on through the stern-tube to the propeller. All this is clearly shown in the illustrations, which also show the wire connections of the magnets and batteries, with a switch screwed to the top of the tube-block. The switch in effect "breaks the wire", thus disconnecting the batteries from the motor. It consists of a small piece of copper or brass moving from "off" side to "on".

The motor should be painted with two coats of good paint on the bare iron of the magnets, and the wire-filled bobbins given a good varnishing with shellac.

The whole boat should also be

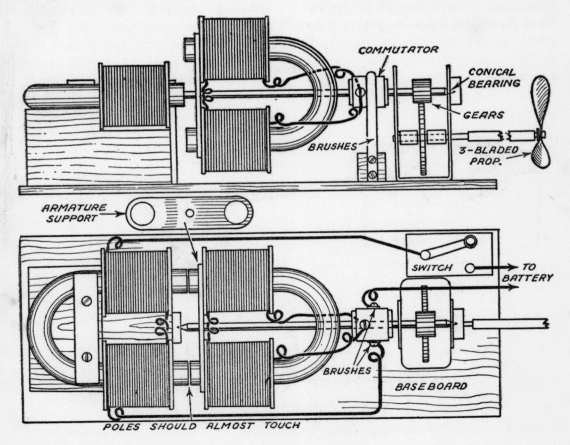

painted or varnished. An electric launch made as described goes at a good speed, and runs as long as switched on—or until the batteries run out, when, of course, they may be replaced with new ones. Keep all moving parts well greased, but avoid grease on the commutator.

Should any difficulty be experienced in getting the motor to run, the connections should be checked carefully and particularly the position of the commutator in relation to the armature, as already explained. The commutator gaps should be in line with the armature-pole pieces. If the motor runs in the reverse direction when first started up, the commutator should be twisted on its shaft (about half a turn) until the desired direction of rotation is obtained. In any case, it is usually an advantage to try slight adjustments to the commutator position. The simplest way is to move the brushes by leaving the mounting-block free at first, so that they can be rotated around the commutator. When the most effective position is found the brushes may be restored to the vertical position, and the commutator moved the equivalent amount.

THE END